Bhagavad Gītā

William Milcetich

Brahmrishi Yoga Publications

Publisher: Brahmrishi Yoga Publications
BrahmrishiYoga.org

Date: December 2014

Printed in United States of America

ISBN: 978-1500915186

For my grandchildren

Contents

Acknowledgement

I am indebted beyond words to my guru, Brahmrishi Vishvatma Bawra, for his acceptance of me, his patient teaching, and his gaze that guided me into my deepest self.

In order to understand the message of the *Bhagavad Gītā*, my guru encouraged me to read the *Gita Rahasaya* of B. G. Tilak. His extensive and authoritative work opened many doorways of comprehension. I have summarized some of Tilak's insights in my introduction. Also, I am indebted to the many translators of the *Bhagavad Gītā*, listed in the Bibliography, whose work I referenced for their English phrasing of this dialogue between Krishna and Arjuna.

For the constant urgings and encouraging voice of my wife, Margot, who prodded me to move beyond my resistance to complete this work, thank you.

I am grateful to Margot, Camille Park, and Lisa Thiel for their helpful suggestions and editing, which enhance the clarity of this presentation.

All proceeds above the cost of printing by Brahmrishi Yoga will be donated to a free school in Jabalpur, India, founded by Brahmrishi Vishvatma Bawra and currently managed by Didi Gyaneshwari. She exemplifies the heart and teaching of our Guru and the dedicated action described in the *Bhagavad Gītā*.

Method of Presentation

My goal is to present what I have learned from Swami Bawra and B. G. Tilak's insights into the *Bhagavad Gītā*. The introduction provides the basic reasoning behind their ideas. Following the introduction is an extended summary of the background from the *Mahābhārta* to explain the circumstances of the civil war. Then the discussion between Krishna and Arjuna is presented—the *Bhagavad Gītā*. In order to orient the reader, each chapter begins with an introduction. I have avoided commentary within the discussion, instead grouping verses with the intent of collating the specific topics Krishna presents to Arjuna.

After much consideration I decided to accept that this discussion took place in the masculine gender between Krishna and Arjuna, two members of the ruling and military elite. Their role was to protect society by fighting in wartime and governing during times of peace. Under these circumstances I did not consider a gender neutral discussion to be appropriate. Yet, the message of the *Bhagavad Gītā* is valuable for every person. Therefore, an attempt was made for inclusivity whenever the discussion lent itself to that.

To assist the English reader with the pronunciation of frequently used Sanskrit terms, letters have been added to the strict transliteration of Sanskrit to English. For example, *citta* is written as *chitta* and *puruśa* as *purusha*. The long vowels of a, i, and u are indicated by the symbols, ā, ī, and ū, sh is indicated by ś, and ya by ñ. I chose to acknowledge and follow the commonly used capitalization for Krishna and all references to Him.

About the Author

It is astonishing for me to look back and examine how a young boy from a small, Midwestern city raised by a strict and practical Catholic family, arrived at the point of preparing a book on the *Bhagavad Gītā*. I resisted this work, telling my wife again and again that more than enough versions already existed and that another would serve no purpose. But a nagging inspiration had awakened in me, that I might share my guru's insight within this epic scripture, and my wife, Margot, prodded me along.

I was born in 1950 to first-generation American parents. My mother was of Italian and Romanian descent and my father was Croatian. My mother was divine in her nature—simple, dedicated and loving. As a child I felt her constant acceptance and loving presence. The year prior to my birth she had carried a baby daughter to full term who was stillborn. Her doctor advised her to heal and postpone another pregnancy. Her priest told her to refrain from using any method of birth control. Consequently, within a short period of time she was pregnant with me, and her loving elation welcomed me into this world.

My father had little opportunity for education because of depression-era poverty. His mother died after bearing six children, and his father sent him, the eldest child, to serve in the Civilian Conservation Corps at the age of seventeen. The missed opportunity for education became a driving force in my father. He ensured that his six children value their Catholic School education. He himself completed his GED and a college degree while working and raising his family.

Both parents were Catholics and, as is common among first generation born of immigrants, religion was the centerpiece of their moral and social life, especially for my father. He was disciplined and hard-working, but also domineering and overbearing. He was determined to see his children advance in society. Firmly entrenched in his religious beliefs and his authority, there was no latitude for questioning his judgment. The rod was never far from his reach.

i

Along with my two sisters and three brothers, I received a traditional Catholic education where I was schooled by nuns, attended Mass, and became an altar boy at the age of ten. I enjoyed the ritual of the Mass and the stage of the altar. But as I entered into my early teen years, my rational mind began to focus on the inconsistencies between the prescribed religious code and the actual behavior of my father and other authority figures. By age twelve, I began to question and to challenge my father's will. My actions created an adversarial environment where disharmony reigned, and I became the "black sheep" of my family. I served as scapegoat for the discord and tension that filled the house. My mother was disturbed during this period, but remained passive. At age sixteen, I severed my relationship with the Catholic Church when a priest attempted to make sexual advances toward me.

Refusing to renounce my viewpoint, I eventually rebelled sufficiently that I was expelled from Catholic School, which was my intention. My father finally relented to my pressure and allowed me to transfer to public school for my senior year. As soon as I graduated from high school I joined the U.S. Navy. This was the beginning of my independence from my father and his values, but I could not yet distance myself from the emotional distress of those early years.

The contentiousness of my relationship with my father continued until his death in 1981. After his death, I found myself still seeking to resolve our differences. The way he perceived me was not how I perceived myself. Many years later, as my meditation practice deepened, I realized that the drama and struggle with my father was my own creation. He was a manifestation of some wrong opinion I carried about my own self. Through this realization, I was able to free myself from the pain and anger I held.

The journey towards realization and liberation is personal and continues over lifetimes. The experiences we encounter become stored as impressions, which form our discriminative ability. These impressions become the basis for our reasoning or our beliefs regarding how we may find meaning in life and attain happiness. The beliefs we hold appear as patterns of behavior or tendencies of liking and disliking and they structure our innate nature and inherent disposition towards life. This is our egoistic self. These impressions, which are the result of our own behaviors, structure the circumstances we encounter life after life.

The liberation of realization comes with the deep understanding that our real Self, our sense of existence, is above all impressions and tendencies. The sense of Self is then realized as inseparably one with an infinite Supreme Source. That Supreme Source is all-pervasive oneness dwelling within us providing a personal experience of divinity. The experience of oneness is called Yoga. Realization does not remove our individuality. We continue to use our intellect, to act with our ego, and to perceive through the mind and senses, but they are now aligned with the benefit of all.

In this message of the *Bhagavad Gītā*, Krishna advises us to pursue Yoga and continue to act for the benefit of all. His disciple, Arjuna, questions whether it is possible to achieve such a goal. Is it worth the effort to attain something so lofty? What if a person begins the practice and then fails to attain success in Yoga? Has such a person wasted his time and life (VI/37-38)? Krishna enjoins him to follow the path. Several births may be needed to achieve realization (VI/45 & VII/19). But no grief comes either in this world, or in the next world (VI/40). No person who performs beneficial actions ever reaches an unhappy end. Having attained the worlds of the doers of meritorious deeds, one is born in the home of the pure and prosperous (VI/41), or may be born in the family of wise *yogis* (VI/42). There, we are united with the knowledge acquired in our former bodies and we can strive onward once more toward perfection. By the momentum of previous practice, we are carried forward even against our will (VI/43). Whatever effort and distance one negotiates on this path is never lost (II/40).

My guru taught us that the dedication to practice in previous lives appears as divine qualities and divine powers in the current life. These come without effort because they are the results of previous practice, and the impressions of practice remain from life to life. This is also taught by Patanjali in the *Yoga Sutras* as part of his discussion on the stages of *Samadhi* (*Yoga Sutras* I/19). The knowledge a practitioner has gained and the methods of practice spontaneously re-emerge. Even the guru will again find the practitioner, because nature arranges the necessary means for a dedicated soul to continue on the path.

My guru, Brahmrishi Vishvatma Bawra (1934-2002) is the founder of the International Brahmrishi Mission. He was born in a small village of India near Varanasi. As a child, he shied away from school and had no formal education. At the age of eighteen, he was enlightened by the touch of a great yogi of the Himalayas, Bhagvan Chandra Mauli, and he remembered many previous lives spent with his guru. Under his guru's guidance, Swami Bawra left his family to study in Ayodhya at the principal center of the Vaishnava Order. There, Swami Bawra studied according to the ancient system of scholarly teaching while performing higher spiritual practices under the guidance of his guru. By this grace of Chandra Mauli, Swami Bawra received a distinctive memory of scripture and philosophical treatises. After a period of time, his master insisted that he return to society and help humanity by teaching the knowledge bestowed by Krishna in the *Bhagavad Gītā*.

Following my time in the military by which I had separated from my family, I returned to Ohio to study at Kent State University for a career as an accountant. All my electives were in psychology and philosophy. I lived in an apartment adjacent to my maternal grandparents' home in the country near the Salem, Ohio branch of the university. I was very close to my grandfather. He loved me dearly and when I was a child he created many opportunities for me to spend time with him away from my father.

I had no knowledge of awakening, of gurus, of Eastern philosophy, of reincarnation, or any such matter. I was an older college student, living a simple life on the G.I bill, and helping my grandparents. After two years of college, I was adapting comfortably to civilian life, but in March of 1974, my plans were interrupted.

I had developed a habit of gazing at the night sky while cruising the ocean on a Navy vessel. At my home in the country, the stars as multiple points of light continued to hold my fascination. Late one evening at my apartment, I felt a strong urge to go outside. That night, after a few minutes of sitting on the grass and looking up, a ball of light, like a comet, descended and entered into the top of my head. It penetrated the full length of my spine and enlightened my whole inner being. At once, I was filled with a luminous essence that dropped me into an experience of complete oneness and pure love—sublime and beyond description. I do not remember how long I stayed there, but only seconds would have sufficed to transform my awareness. After I came back to my senses, I was stunned and revitalized. I felt completely renewed, better than I had ever felt.

This was my introduction to my guru in this lifetime. But I had no knowledge of him. At this time, I had no framework for explaining what had happened to me. Though the experience was transformative, I was also disturbed. I wanted some way of giving meaning to the experience.

Over the next few months I would periodically feel as if lifted outside of myself, or what I normally thought of as myself. I might be mowing the grass or taking a walk when suddenly my awareness would expand beyond the body. I felt as if I were sitting on the top of my head rather dwelling inside my body. I was sitting in a great space of freedom that was exhilarating and joyful, but I was unsure of what was going on. These experiences were unbidden. I had no control. I applied no effort. The experience would come and go. Fortunately, I always returned to my senses and my everyday abilities, so I could continue with my life.

I began in earnest to seek explanations. I prayed for understanding. I sat quietly in contemplation. I read the Bible from cover to cover. I read Carlos Castaneda's *The Teaching of Don Juan*. I came across a woman who had studied with the Rosicrucian's and she became a sounding board with whom I could safely express myself. Finally I came across the *Autobiography of a Yogi* by Paramahansa Yoganda, and I began to feel less crazy. But I still did not feel at ease with the expansive experience.

When in August, 1974 my grandfather died, I was taken aback. This was my first experience of losing someone close to me. To calm the turbulence of my grief, I walked alone for hours at a time. When it was time to start classes again, I was reluctant to continue. I followed the easy route of filling my schedule with electives, but I was aimless and unsure of how to move forward.

In December, 1974, another defining and unimaginable experience occurred that set my path on course. During final exams, I was studying in my apartment when I began to feel tugged or pulled. I was alone, so it made no sense. It was as if my mental energy was being torn outside of my body. The intensity was so strong that I feared I was being attacked by some negative force. I sat down cross-legged on the floor of my room and began to pray. Suddenly from the base of my spine a light shot upward and out the top of my head. A cone of light formed around me protecting me from the force I was feeling; it could not penetrate this light. I sat quietly and the force appeared to depart. I felt comforted, and, after some time, stood up and left the house in order to put some distance between me and the incident.

The next day at the university, I felt more normal in a political theory class that included the study of the early Greek philosophers. In this class I was introduced to Socrates, Aristotle, and Plato, in particular to the allegory of the cave which had become important to me. The philosophy was inspiring and I initiated many class discussions. After class, a woman I barely knew asked me to help her study for the upcoming exam. I agreed. But when we got to the library, her disposition changed. She wanted to go where we could be alone. We ended up at my apartment.

Then she changed even more, and began to offer me power and the opportunity for wealth. She acted flirtatious and then withdrew and continued to talk about power and wealth. I was confused and told her harshly that I wanted nothing of what she was offering. Once I was firm with her, her disposition changed again. She settled into herself and began to speak quietly.

She thanked me for my decision, and told me she was aware of my experience the prior evening. I had said nothing of it to her, yet she continued to explain how the entity that had challenged me had entered her. She was acting upon its wishes. This had happened to her once before, and had I not resisted, the negative energy would have created suffering in our lives. She then gave me some advice: Firstly, I should begin a meditation practice, and secondly, I should move to Youngstown, Ohio.

Shortly thereafter, a friend told me of a teacher of Transcendental Meditation (TM). I immediately went to an introductory lecture and signed up for instruction. I observed the ritual ceremony and then received a mantra, a simple sound to repeat in meditation that was related with Mother Goddess. When I received the mantra and began to meditate, energy burst from the base of my spine and up through the top of my head like a bolt of lightning. My spine, neck and head became rigid. Unable to move, I was filled from within by a divine light.

Within one month I left my home in Salem, tossing away my last cigarette as I stepped into my car to drive to Maharishi International University for study and extended meditation practice. There I was introduced to the Science of Creative Intelligence, an explanation of the principal existence of consciousness and energy. We meditated several times a day and practiced yoga postures and breathing exercises. Here I felt comfortable and fully adopted a vegetarian diet. I knew I was moving in the right direction.

I was not ready to return to my life after one month, and so signed up for an additional three-month training course. This was the first phase of becoming a TM teacher. The course included extra meditation time, as well as more yoga postures, breathing exercises, and videotaped lectures of Maharishi Mahesh Yogi.

Following four months of study, I finally returned to Ohio to prepare for the move to Youngstown. I decided to trust the message I had received, and continued my college studies at Youngstown State University. I first shared an apartment with friends, but after three months I was invited to move into the TM center. I helped the teachers by giving introductory lectures on meditation, answering questions from new students, and helping students become comfortable with the process of meditation.

I had decided to take the final phase of teacher training, but because I was a new meditator, the organization recommended that I wait nine months between the two phases. So, I made plans to take the course that would begin in July, 1976, in France. I was continuing to have extraordinary experiences both in and out of meditation. I was less interested in my college studies and more interested in practice. During this time, I concentrated on meditation, prayer and the study of religion and philosophy.

In the spring of 1976 a new development came into my meditation practice. Whenever I closed my eyes to meditate I was instantly filled with divine light and fell in deep communion with what I considered to be God. In prayer I felt I could communicate directly with this presence. I felt God was my best friend. Then my meditations changed. I would enter into the light, and the light would take the form of a man with a white beard dressed in orange cloth. Sitting in a cross-legged position, he gazed deeply into my being. We would sit for the whole meditation in complete communion. I did not know who this person was, but this became my daily practice.

The experience continued for months. The man in orange became my best friend, the best friend that I could ever have. I felt so much love and compassion. There was no separation between us. Any question or doubt

I had would melt in front of him. I came to trust him completely, but most importantly, I was happy.

After some time he gave me a new mantra. This was confusing for me. I was a TM practitioner and having good experiences with the mantra I had received. Reluctant to change, I initiated my meditation with my TM mantra, but when it would mutate into this new mantra, I would not resist.

Naturally, my thoughts turned to how I could fully devote myself to meditation and philosophy. Becoming a monk in the Christian tradition did not make sense. So, I just carried on studying, meditating, praying, and enjoying my new spiritual friend.

In early July of 1976 the reason for moving to Youngstown, Ohio revealed itself. While I was enjoying my practice and thinking of becoming a monk, my future wife, Margot, appeared. Margot was studying at Maharishi International University in Iowa and was on her way home to Philadelphia for summer vacation. Youngstown was on the highway to Philadelphia.

While traveling with friends, their vehicle broke down in Gary, Indiana. She and a friend hitched a ride on a semi-truck, but when the driver stopped at a truck stop in Youngstown, a motherly dispatch woman prevented her from going any further. She insisted that Margot find another way to travel.

As a TM teacher, Margot knew she could contact any center, and she knew a person from her teacher training who now lived in Youngstown. She found the number of the center in the phone book hanging by a wire in the booth and made the call. Another friend who was living at the center answered the phone and was happy to retrieve her from the truck stop. They returned to where I was living. I was out, and when I returned, was informed that we had a guest in the spare room on the third floor where I stayed. But I had no contact with her as she had already settled in for the night.

The next morning while I was fixing my breakfast and preparing to leave the house, Margot came into the kitchen. We greeted each other and I offered to make her breakfast. I asked her if she would be willing to be a substitute for my afternoon activity of helping new students with their meditations. I was going to be busy taking three children on an outing. She agreed and I left for the day.

Throughout the day my thoughts turned to marriage and children. This was surprising, but I assumed that enjoying the day's activities with three children must have stimulated the feeling. When I returned to the center no one was home and I decided to go and visit a friend. He was not home, but I discovered Margot there, visiting with her friend who was married to mine. We stayed and talked for some time and then I offered to give Margot a ride back to the center.

At the center, I visited with a housemate, and Margot went directly to her room. After some time, I went upstairs to settle into my regular routine of meditation and prayer. Strangely, when I began to meditate, my orange-clad friend told me to marry this woman. I was stunned and began arguing with him. I prayed harder, trying to dislodge these thoughts. No matter how earnestly I prayed and said my mantra, the thought would not depart. Finally, I set up an ultimatum: if I am to marry this person, have her come immediately to knock on my door; otherwise, I will be a monk.

I thought this would work because it was unlikely she would come to my door at midnight. To my surprise, almost immediately a knock came on my door. I was dumbfounded. "Who is it?" I said gruffly. "Margot," replied the visitor. "What do you want?" I asked.

I could not believe what was happening to me. How could this person come to my room at this time of night? She hardly knew me. She was asleep in the room across the hall, or so I thought. But she was not asleep. She was having an abnormally expansive experience of her own ending in a vision that had frightened her. She wanted to talk to someone, and she chose me. I was trapped. From behind the door, I told her to wait while I dressed. Then we went out in the summer night to walk. We strolled to a swing set in a park where we sat and talked for a long time. I questioned her about God, organized religion, meditation, food, and such. I was satisfied by her answers, but did not reveal the source of my keen interest.

Upon returning to the center, I lay awake for hours. I could not believe what happened. I continued my debate with the voice inside. Could I continue to follow my chosen path? This was my challenge.

I had arranged to take a friend to the airport the next day. I decided to go from there to my grandparents' house. No one was living there as my father was remodeling it in preparation for his retirement. There I could take time to contemplate this change of events.

When Margot heard I was driving her friend to the airport, she asked to go along. I reluctantly agreed and thought I could leave her off at the center before continuing south to Leetonia. On the way back from the airport, I told her my plans to spend a few days in the country. She asked if she could come. I tried to discourage her, but she would not be dissuaded. She said she loved the country and wanted to see the home. She insisted she would be like a sister, nothing more. I reluctantly agreed.

When we arrived, I showed her around, and we threw down two mattresses in separate rooms. Then we both lay awake. Neither of us could sleep. She called out to ask if I would like to walk. It was once again midnight as we set out down the cobble-stone road that led to the nearby town of Leetonia. We talked for a long time, and finally, I shared my experience with her and asked what she thought. She took my hand and said it was her hope to find her husband this year. So, before the walk was over, we agreed to marry.

We returned to the center to stay for a few days. I was leaving for France to complete the TM teacher training within ten days, so I agreed to take Margot to her home in Philadelphia and then depart from there. We set our wedding date for the following December, 1976, after my return from France, and agreed to not speak of it to anyone, including her mother. When we arrived in Philadelphia, her mother was out for the evening. I went to bed and Margot stayed up to greet her. Naturally she could not keep quiet. The next morning I found myself being interrogated by her mother and step-father. Margot and I were married in December 20, 1976.

Between 1976 and 1982, I finished my studies and started my career in Akron, Ohio, during which time we had two sons. My life was settling down and my subtle experiences quieted. In hindsight, I believe my guru allowed for an interval of time where I might stabilize my life in the world. Margot and I meditated regularly, kept to a vegetarian diet, and began remodeling a starter home near Kent, encountering new struggles and meeting challenges in our new life as a married couple and a family.

In March, 1982, I was at work when a friend called with an invitation to join him in visiting an Indian saint in Cleveland. This was frowned upon by the TM movement, so I called Margot to see what she thought. She agreed that I should go after work. When I arrived at the apartment where the man was staying, I was stunned. There sat the orange-robed man who had appeared to me again and again in meditation. I could not believe it. He smiled, told me to sit down, and take some food. I told him I did not come for food and did not want to waste my time eating. He laughed heartily. He said, "There is plenty of time. Don't worry, I will answer all of your questions and remove all of your doubt." I ate and we talked for hours.

The next morning I went back to see him. He took me up to his room to give me a guru mantra. It was the same mantra he had given to me in meditation six years before. He smiled in recognition. That same evening, Margot and the boys came with me. After that meeting, we went every evening, following him from house to house for the recitation of the Ramayana and lectures in Hindi. We spent every spare moment with him, finding time to talk in the afternoons when he was free.

At the end of this first stay, he told us he would return to Ohio in late summer, and would live in our house for a month. We agreed. He wanted to reach out to Americans and was looking for his disciples. We rushed to complete the remodeling of our small home, and then hosted our teacher. We invited people for meditation and philosophy, and he invited them to join us for meals. This was challenging for Margot who was home with two children under the age of five, and for me, who was off to work early in the morning after staying up late to sit with my guru. And yet, we were inspired by his presence and his careful teaching, and enjoyed his simplicity and divine nature.

The following year our guru again stayed with us for a month. He wanted to establish a center in the Cleveland area. During this second visit, he convinced me to come to India. In January 1984, I began the first of my travels to India. I stayed at my guru's main ashram and traveled with him and a group of his followers for five weeks. One night at the ashram my guru again came to me in subtle form while I was meditating. He stood at the top of a set of stairs; I was at the bottom. He called me by my soul's name, which I had not yet heard. When I looked up to him, a mirror appeared in front of me and no longer seeing him, I saw my own face. Then, one by one, numerous faces of all the lives we had shared came into the mirror. I recognized each face as myself. Each person was the changing outer form of my immortal soul. This experience removed any doubt I may have had regarding reincarnation and the continuity of our existence.

In 1992, I returned to India in response to a strong urge to return to a Mother Goddess Temple. The temple I went to was in a small cave on the side of Vindhyachal Mountain. Over the years, after meditation, I had developed the habit of writing in a journal to Mother Goddess as I worked through subtle experiences. Now, after visiting the shrine, my guru greeted me aloud for the first time with the name of Yogendra, the same name he had used in 1984 to show me my previous lives. He told me my name was associated with this temple of Ashta Bhuja, eight-limbed Mother Goddess. The eight limbs represent intellect, ego, mind, and the five elements of earth, water, fire, air and space. The name is a reminder to remain in yoga and be a master of these gifts.

I made this second journey to India just after my wife returned from her first trip in 1992. Early in our marriage my wife and I decided that I would pursue a career, and she would be free to teach yoga and meditation and care for our two sons. Margot completed a master's degree after marriage when she realized she would continue teaching yoga and meditation as a profession. In 2005, she founded Brahmrishi Yoga Teacher Training, a school that incorporates Kapil's Sāmkhya philosophy as its base. Her inspiration to teach Sāmkhya was initiated by Swami Bawra's insistence that the philosophy would best suit the Western mind. On her journey to India, he had named her after the mother of Kapil, Devhuti, as a way to guide her development.

Swami Bawra encouraged me, now Yogendra, to remain in my professional career as an accountant while continuing to meditate, study, and support Margot, now Devhuti, in her teaching. And together, for many years, we have held meditation and philosophy sessions based on the teachings of Swami Bawra. We studied annually with him when he traveled to the United States, Canada, and England, and periodically traveled to India to study. In 2006, I retired from my professional career and devoted myself to compiling the philosophy in texts for students of the school, beginning with Sāmkhya and Yoga.

Marriage has many challenges. Spiritual growth is not easy. Awakening to a deeper sense of self does not mean one's learning is over. Margot has written a memoir called "Cloud Cover" that covers much of the history of her growth and our time with our guru. The mid-1990's was a culminating time of struggle when Margot chose to separate from me for a six-month trial period. I was left to raise two middle school boys while working full time. Although very painful, I learned a lot during this period—most importantly, how to let go and let be. Reconciliation occurred and we were able to continue forward.

I have come to understand how my early spiritual awakening was merely a first step in my search for truth. I needed to gain more knowledge and experience, which required many years of persistent effort, encouraged by the grace of my guru. And although I wanted to be away from my duties to accomplish this goal, my guru strongly advocated that I remain with my responsibilities. He urged me to be stable in the thick of commotion and chaos. At times I was deeply challenged, but with his inspiration I continued working and raising a family, while proceeding with spiritual practice.

In time I came to realize that I had been trying to cast away my own existence in order to be with God. This misguided effort was embodied in the struggle with my father. My father was a manifestation of my own wrong inclination to destroy, eliminate, or cast out my own ego self. No matter how hard he tried to diminish me, I resisted. And I found that in meditation, no amount of surrender could dissolve my ego. I came to accept my ego as a divine gift: a means to experience eternal bliss and an instrument for serving the Infinite Source.

This transformed my relationship with God and life. Each time I offered my self into God, God would give my self back to me. I began to realize the true meaning of my mantra: the Infinite Source is my own existence, and the impulse of I-am is His[1] means to live in the world. I could reside within Him if I accepted that the sense of existence or my own sense of "I" was His medium for interacting with the world.

As this realization settled within me, my internal struggle with my father ended, releasing me from the bondage of anger. I learned to honor and accept my own individual existence as the means for my relationship with God and as a manifestation of God in life, thus ending the need to destroy this gift of existence.

Individual existence is a divine gift, offering one the ability to experience the Supreme and be in an immanent relationship with the Supreme. It is through our I-amness that we have a direct experience of our Divine Source. The Supreme is both transcendent and immanent.

---

[1] The masculine is used here to designate consciousness as the opposed to the feminine, which designates energy. The supreme source is inclusive of both.

Our individual I-amness and this Supreme Source are one, and the highest attainment of human life is realizing that our I-amness is a manifestation of this Supreme Source. I and my Father are one.

The instrument of the ego is not an illusion, nor is it our true sense of existence. It is the doer, the performer of action on behalf of the Supreme. We are not this doer; the doer is merely an innocent projection and an agent of our belief system. The impressions we hold in our intellect, the thinking process itself, is what makes us limited and bound. Re-orienting our thinking to include the understanding of how we are instruments of one Source sets us free to enjoy immortality. Likewise, our mind and senses are great instruments and gifts of divinity. It is not the instrument itself that is bad or defective, but the misguided direction and misuse of these instruments based on our beliefs.

Our beliefs are formed by the impressions of our experience. These impressions are not permanent and are subject to change. One treasured belief that most of us mistakenly hold is that the body is the base of human existence. The first objective of yoga is to move beyond body consciousness, to separate your sense of self from the objects around you, including the body, and to unite your self with the higher sense of Self, or soul, within. This is Yoga.

The *Bhagavad Gītā* is a treatise on yoga. The primary aim of Krishna's teaching is to help Arjuna understand his inner essence and how his lower nature, including the intellect, the ego, the mind, and the senses are supportive and not determinative of his existence. This process is similar to the shift that humanity went through over many centuries as the discovery and realization dawned that the earth is not the center of the universe, but rather orbits around the sun. Even though the idea is generally accepted, we continue to use language indicating that the sun rises and sets around us. It might serve us to appreciate how our earth and its inhabitants continually turn to greet the sun in the morning and rotate away in the evening.

Now the heliocentric concept is well established, but it was a tremendous struggle for philosophers and scientists to posit a new idea. Likewise, for thousands of years, great teachers have come to help us understand that our bodies and senses cannot define the purpose of our existence. Satisfying the fleeting desires of the body, senses and mind is not enough. The control of the ego will break down. The intellect can misguide us. We have an immortal soul that is on an eternal journey. The gifts of our body, senses, mind, ego and intellect are supportive, not determinative. Through quieting ourselves in meditation and seeking deeply within to find union with our Source, we can find a way to transform our impressions and use our gifts to serve life. In this way we can enjoy the tranquility and bliss of union with the Supreme Source and perform action free from bondage and suffering. This is the message and teaching of the *Bhagavad Gītā*.

Introduction

The vision of my guru Brahmrishi Vishvatma Bawra (1934 to 2002) is my guiding influence, both in my personal practice and in my writing. Although he chose to live the life of a *sanyāsi*, a renunciant, he was nevertheless an active person. And he encouraged his disciples who took the vow of *sanyās* to complete advanced college degrees in order to serve humanity. They are now, effectively running various schools and centers. No matter where he was, he lectured daily on Indian philosophy—including the *Bhagavad Gītā*. While many of his lectures were compiled into books in both Hindi and English, he had no English commentary on the *Bhagavad Gītā* for our use. When we asked him which *Gītā* we should read, he invariably recommended Lokmanya Tilak's *Gītā Rahasya*.

While in India in 1994, I acquired a copy of the *Gītā Rahasya*. I brought the large volume home where it sat on a shelf for many years. The book was daunting—half the book consisted of an introduction to Tilak's position. My work and family life were demanding during those years. Eventually upon my retirement from a professional career in 2006, I returned to my love of Indian philosophy. I would immerse myself, diving into Tilak's thought only after helping my wife prepare texts for her Yoga school, Brahmrishi Yoga. To create a text that captured our guru's insights on Sāmkhya and Yoga, I revisited our collection of our guru's lectures, gathered over twenty years, searched out additional lectures from other centers, and began to compile and edit his material into books. The first was Sāmkhya's Tattva Samāsa, followed by a commentary on the Yoga Sūtras, and the Katha, Māndūkya and Īśa Upanishads. During this time, I began teaching meditation to Margot's students and community members, presenting philosophy based on Swami Bawra's insights and my own experience.

Brahmrishi Yoga's advanced training included a study of the teachings of the *Bhagavad Gītā*. As we explored different versions, we were repeatedly disenchanted with translations that appeared to alter the meaning of Krishna's words to Arjuna. Additionally, the commentaries did not express the unique perspective we had been taught by our guru. In 2010, we compiled aspects of Bawra's viewpoint into *Yoga in Action*. This small volume contained teachings from the third and fourth chapters of the *Gītā*. Finally in 2012, I delved into Tilak's *Gītā Rahasya* and discovered a wealth of understanding and perspective that substantiated my disillusionment with other commentaries and helped me to formulate my own thought.

Lokmanya Tilak (1856-1920) lived during the time the Indian people were beginning their stand of independence against the British rule. A patriot and leading politician, he was renowned as a scholar, philosopher, lawyer, journalist, educator, and social reformer. He acted as the first leader of the Indian Independence Movement. British authorities called him the "Father of Indian unrest." Lokmanya was not his given name; it was conferred as an honorary title meaning "accepted by the people as their leader." Tilak's *Gītā Rahasya* was written during a six year period when he was imprisoned by the British.

In his article, "How I came to write the *Gītā Rahasya*,[2]" Tilak presented his reasons for writing a different interpretation of the *Gītā*.

> I had occasion to read from time to time the Sanskrit commentaries and other criticisms, as also the expositions by many learned scholars in English and in Marathi on the *Gītā*.

> I was then faced by the doubt as to why the *Gītā*, which was expounded in order to induce Arjuna, who was dejected by the idea that it was a sin to war with one's own relatives, to fight, should contain only an exposition of the manner in which release could be obtained by knowledge (*jnana*) or by devotion (*bhakti*), and that doubt gradually gained ground because I could not find a satisfactory answer to that question in any commentary on the *Gītā*.

> It is quite possible that others too might have felt the same doubt. One cannot say *no* to that. When a person is engulfed in commentaries and he cannot find a different solution, he may feel that the solution given in the commentary is not satisfactory.

---

[2] Bhavan's Journal Vol XIX No. 7, Diwali Number 1972, pp. 131-135.

Introduction

I, therefore, put aside all criticisms and commentaries, and independently and thoughtfully read the *Gītā* over several times.

I then got out of the clutches of the commentators and was convinced that the original *Gītā* did not preach the Philosophy of Renunciation (*nivṛtti*), but of Energism (Karma Yoga); and that possibly, the single word Yoga used in the *Gītā* had been used to mean Karma Yoga.

The *Gītā* was not preached either as a pastime for persons tired out after living a worldly life in the pursuit of selfish motives nor as a preparatory lesson for living such worldly life; it was preached in order to give philosophical advice as to how one should live his worldly life with an eye to release and to teach the true duty of human beings in worldly life.

My last prayer to everyone, therefore, is that one should not fail to thoroughly understand this ancient science of the life of a householder, or of worldly life, as early as possible in one's life.

Many of the great seers of the ancient Vedas lived as householders. In two of the most important epics of India, the *Ramāyana* and the *Mahābharata*, Rama and Krishna, both the incarnations of Godhead, live as householders and manage kingdoms. Why then would Krishna teach that this active lifestyle is inferior to renunciation and that a vigorous life is a mere stepping stone to renouncing the world?

In the preface to *Gītā Rahasya*, Tilak presents his view that the principal subject matter of the *Gītā* is not an explanation of the differing paths of knowledge and devotion. Nor is the text a justification of the idea that worldly action is inferior to both renunciation and devotion, and that as such, it should be abandoned. Clearly these two paths of knowledge and devotion were discussed by Krishna. The primary duty of every human being is to gain intimate knowledge of the Supreme in order to purify the intellect and gain emancipation. Devotion to this source is a natural consequence of pure knowledge. Tilak's view is that knowledge and devotion are supportive of a life of vigorous action, which is in no way an inferior life.

The *Gītā* does not segregate life into the secular and the sacred, but presents a unified philosophy of human life called Yoga. Swami

3

Ranganathananda (1908 to 2005), the 13th President of the Ramakrishna Mission, explained that Vedanta advocates the practice of inward contemplation as a means of creating stability while acting in the external world. Both action and meditation are necessary for our well-being. One without the other does not lead to a healthy individual or society. Through outward action a well-ordered society is maintained, and through inward contemplation a value-oriented life is established. Inward contemplation is needed for peace and balance which, by enhancing our feelings of fulfillment and connection with others, develops our capacity to love. Both contemplation and action are essential to the health of every member of society. In his introduction to the *Bhagavad Gītā*, Swami Ranganathananda tells us:

> In the past, people mostly read the *Gītā* as a pious act, and for a little peace of mind. We never realized that this is a book of intense practicality, that this is the greatest book of practical Vedanta capable of helping us to create a society of fully developed human beings. We never understood the practical application of the *Gītā* teachings. If we had done so, we would not have had the thousand years of foreign invasions, internal caste conflicts, feudal oppressions, and mass poverty. We never took the *Gītā* seriously, but now we have to. We need a philosophy that can help us to build a new welfare society, based on human dignity, freedom and equality...Śri Krishna gave it several thousand years ago as a practical philosophy, but we converted it into a mere book of piety.
>
> [The teaching of the *Gītā*] is not meant merely to give peace of mind; it is a comprehensive philosophy of life and work...for realizing spiritual reality while maintaining humanistic objectives.

The message of the *Gītā* is intended to inspire us to work for the good of all. In the opening of the fourth chapter Krishna describes how he gave this philosophy of Yoga to society's leaders, so that through its instruction they would become strong and capable of serving and protecting a society that nourishes its individuals. Krishna continued by saying that this teaching is not new. It is taught continually in every age, providing for emancipation while establishing the value of vigor and action. The cornerstone of his teaching is the performance of action without selfish

4

motive, and without hope for personal gain or a specific outcome. We have the right to work, but we do not have the ability to control the results. We should fulfill our responsibilities according to our skills, capabilities and current status in life.

In his lengthy introduction to the *Bhagavad Gītā*, Tilak addresses the roots of the difficulty in its interpretation. An historical survey of the problem will help us understand his reasoning. Vedanta philosophy is supported by three sources: the Upanishads, *Vedanta Sūtras*, and the *Bhagavad Gītā*. Vedanta means "the end of the Veda." The Upanishads are a collection of enunciations of the great seers, accounts of their realizations regarding the Supreme Self, the manifested world, and the individual self. Because the Upanishads were written by different seers they contain different thoughts that are at times contradictory. Thus, the *Vedanta Sūtras* were written to harmonize these positions. The teachings of the Upanishads and *Vedanta Sūtras* were primarily ascetical. The exposition of the *Bhagavad Gītā*, however, provided a practical philosophy of an active engagement with life, but this intention was distorted to support the bias of renunciation and devotion preached by the schools of Vedanta.

It was a common practice for the *ācāryas*, teachers, of different subsets of Vedanta to write commentaries on these three pillars of Vedanta, the Upanishads, the *Vedanta Sūtras* and the *Bhagavad Gītā*, in order to establish the authority of their position. Most well-known is *advaita*, the non-dualism of Śamkarācārya. His philosophy is dominant in most commentaries. Countering his position was *visistādvaita*, qualified monism, taught by Rāmānujācārya. The third is the philosophy of *dvaita*, duality, of Madhvacarya. Additional subsets of the Vedanta school exist, but these three are predominant. According to Tilak, "although the *Bhagavad Gītā* supports only one theme it has come to be believed that the same *Bhagavad Gītā* supports all the various doctrines."

Commentaries that pre-date Śamkarācārya's are not available, therefore that commentary, dating from the early ninth century, is considered primary. Śamkarācārya references earlier commentaries that had proposed an energetic interpretation of the *Bhagavad Gītā*. But any philosophy that supported the importance of action blended with spiritual knowledge was not acceptable to him. He refuted the doctrine that stated that every person who acquires spiritual knowledge ought to continue to perform duties appropriate to their skills, abilities, and particular status in life as long as they live. Subsequent commentaries followed Śaṃkarācārya's interpretation and reiterated his belief that action was a preliminary path, inferior to a reclusive life of contemplation.

Every system of Vedic thought has both a theoretical and a practical aspect. The philosophical aspect explains the nature of truth in a scientific and logical way, and the practical aspect prescribes the mode of life that is the means for attaining the goal of liberation or release. According to Tilak,

> Śaṃkarācārya (788 to 820) says that (1) the multiplicity of the various objects in the world, such as I, you and all other things which are visible to the eye, is not a true multiplicity, but that there is in all of them a single, pure, and eternal *Parabrahman* [Supreme Self], and various human organs experience multiplicity as a result of a *māyā* [illusion] of that *Parabrahman*. (2) The *Ātman* [self] of man is also fundamentally of the same nature as this [Supreme Self]; and (3) that it is not possible for any one to obtain release except after the complete realization or personal experience of this identity of the *Ātman* and the *Parabrahman*.
>
> This is known as non-dualism because the sum and substance of this doctrine is, that there is no other independent and real substance except one pure self-enlightened, eternal *Parabrahman*; that the multiplicity which is visible to the eyes is an optical illusion or an imaginary experience resulting from the effect of illusion or *māyā*; and that *māyā* is not some distinct, real, or independent substance, but is *mithyā* [unreal].
>
> [Coupled with this philosophical doctrine is the suggested mode of life.] Although it is necessary to perform the actions pertaining to the state of a householder in order to acquire the capacity of realizing the identity of the *Brahman* with *Ātman* by the purification of the mind, yet it is impossible to obtain release unless one discontinues those actions later on and ultimately gives them up and takes on asceticism; because in as much as action and knowledge are mutually antagonistic like light and darkness, the knowledge of a man does not become perfect unless a man has entirely conquered all root tendencies and given up action.

This is the path of renunciation. An aspirant is expected to give up action and remain steeped in knowledge or contemplation of the Supreme Self. Śamkarācārya and his followers espouse the view that the *Bhagavad Gītā* is not in favor of the synthesis of knowledge and action that was prescribed by the early commentators. Instead, their arguments attempt to prove that Krishna supported a doctrine of renunciation of action.

About 250 years later, Rāmānuja (1016 to 1137), founded the school of *visistādvaita*, qualified non-dualism or qualified monism, which countered the doctrine of illusion, non-dualism and renunciation. *Visistādvaita* literally means *ādvaita* with qualifications. One Supreme is a qualified whole. The Supreme is characterized as having attributes or expressions, but is a unified whole. The diverse expression of its attributes is subsumed in an underlying unity.

Tilak describes Rāmānuja's position as follows: "Although the *jīva* [individual being], the cosmos, and *Īsvara* [Godhead] were independent, yet in as much as *jīva*, individual beings, and the cosmos are both the body of one and the same *Īsvara*, therefore the bodied *Īsvara* is one and one alone and that out of this subtle…the numerous forms of life and cosmos came into existence." My guru would describe how the one includes the many through the example of the sun. Individual rays of light are like individual beings; and the combined rays of light are the cosmos. Both are as part and parcel of the one form of the sun.

Rāmānuja did not include the Yoga of action as described by Krishna, but, according to Tilak, that "although knowledge, action and devotion are all three referred to in the *Gītā*, the doctrine enunciated is the essence of qualified monism [that of] devotion to Vasudevā [Krishna] for the mode of life." Essentially, Rāmānuja changed the non-dual philosophy to qualified monism and substituted devotion for renunciation as the message of the *Gītā*. He said: "…yet if devotion is looked upon as the highest duty of man from the point of view of the mode of life, then the lifelong performance of the worldly duties pertaining to one's particular status becomes an inferior mode of life; and on that account the interpretation…favors renunciation of action."

Thus, whether one remains steeped in contemplation of the Supreme Self or devoted to a form of the Supreme, according to both non-dual and qualified monism Vedanta, one must denounce action. And on that account Rāmānuja's interpretation must be looked upon as favoring renunciation of action. Tilak continues, "The same objection applies to the other cults which came into existence after the date of Rāmānujācārya. Although Rāmānujācārya may have been right in saying that the theory of the non-reality or illusion is wrong and that one ultimately attains release only by devotion...yet looking upon the *Parabrahman* and the conscious ego as one with the source and also different in other ways is a contradiction in terms and inconsistent."

A third school came into existence in the 13th Century to address this inconsistency between the Supreme Self and the conscious ego, the doctrine of duality of Madhvācārya (1197 to 1276). Tilak summaries Madhvācārya's commentary on the *Gītā* saying, "although desireless action has been extolled in the *Gītā*, yet desireless action is only a means and devotion is the true and ultimate cult, and that when once one has become perfect by following the path of devotion, whether one thereafter performs or does not perform action is just the same."

Tilak then concludes:

> No one can entertain any doubt that these various *ācāryas* who wrote the commentaries were learned, religious and extremely pure-minded. Then why should there have been a difference...The *Gītā* is not such a pot of jugglery that any one can extract any meaning he likes out of it. The *Gītā* was written long before these various schools of thought came into existence, and it was preached by Śri Krishna to Arjuna not to increase his confusion, but to remove it; and it contains a preaching of one definite creed to Arjuna (*Gītā* 5.1 & 2) and the effect of that advice on Arjuna has also been what it ought to have been...

> However numerous the different cults...may be, yet with the exception of a few specified things, such as the *Īsvara*, conscious ego, and the cosmos and their mutual interrelations, all other things are common to all the various cults; and therefore in the various doctrinal commentaries or criticisms which have been written on our authoritative religious texts, ninety per cent of the statement or stanza in the original work are interpreted in more or less the same way. The only difference is as regards the remaining statements or doctrines. If these statements are taken in their literal meaning, they cannot possibly be equally appropriate to

all the cults. Therefore, different commentators, who have propounded different doctrines, usually accept as important only such of these statements as are consistent with their own particular cult, and either say that the others are unimportant, or skillfully twist the meanings of such statements…or wherever possible, they draw hidden meanings or inferences favorable to themselves from easy and plain statements, and say the particular work is an authority for their particular cult.

Tilak then gives us the prescribed method for determining the message of a book. This method is an old and generally accepted rule stated in a verse by the Mīmāmsā writers.[3] Seven factors are given for considering the purport of any writing. The first two factors are offered to the reader at the beginning and ending of the work. What is the motive and conclusion of the writer? The third is the consistent position taken throughout the book, a clear proposition repeated over and over again. The fourth and fifth factors address what is new and the effect of that knowledge. The sixth factor to consider is how the author covers additional topics as the occasion arises by way of illustration or comparison in the course of argument. In the sixth factor we look for consistency, similarities or differences that support his ideas. These discussions are supplemental edification. Finally, the seventh factor is the refutation of contrary positions.

The *Bhagavad Gītā* was preached by Krishna to Arjuna at the onset of a civil war between the cousin clans of the Kauravas and the Pāndavas. Krishna was giving encouragement to a dejected Arjuna who was on the point of renouncing the world. Krishna did not support Arjuna's renunciation; rather, he was enjoining him to perform his duties as a *kṣatriya*, a warrior. The code of the *kṣatriya* was to fight, but Arjuna was emotionally conflicted by his devotion to his ancestors and preceptors and his affection for his relatives. Tilak says, "Śri Krishna did not intend to send Arjuna to the woods as a mendicant by making a *sanyasi* [renunciant] of him, filling his mind with apathy, or to induce him to go to the Himalayas as a *yogin* wearing a loin cloth and eating the leaves of the *nim*

---

[3] Pūrva Mīmāmsā is one of the six schools of Indian Philosophy, whose primary inquiry is into the nature of *dharma* (behaviors that uphold life). According to the school, these behaviors are not founded on reason or observation, but determined by revelation in the Vedas.

tree. Nor did the Blessed Lord intend to place in his hands cymbals and a drum…and make him into a devotee and chant and dance for the Lord." Again and again Krishna stated reasons Arjuna must act and fight. And at the end of the discourse, Krishna again reiterated that it is best that one act, and perform action with a disinterested state of mind.

Tilak emphasizes,

> There is no doubt that the knowledge of the absolute Self included in the path of renunciation is faultless; and that the equability of reason or the desireless state of mind, produced by it is acceptable to and admitted by the *Gītā*. Nevertheless, the opinion of [this] school that one must entirely abandon action in order to obtain release is not acceptable to the *Gītā*…
>
> The most important doctrine laid down by the *Gītā* is even after…[realization] perform all the activities of life, with the …the feeling of indifference to the world and the equability of [reason], which results from the realization of the [Supreme Self].

According to Tilak, the crucial question of the *Bhagavad Gītā* is *to act or not to act*. Should we remove ourselves from participating in society and renounce all actions after self-realization, or should we continue to act without selfish motive, using our developed skills and abilities for the well-being of the world? The *Bhagavad Gītā* favors choosing activity. And Krishna opens the discussion with Arjuna with a description of the two paths. Sāmkhya, the path of knowledge while abstaining from action, and Yoga, the path of disinterested or desireless action. He will clarify and separate these two teachings for Arjuna, highlight that both paths will lead to realization, and emphasize in his opinion that the path of Yoga is the better and more worthy of the two.

We will see in the background discussion from the *Mahābhārata*, the epic containing the *Bhagavad Gītā*, Arjuna's conflict and confusion developed as a result of the diplomatic efforts that occurred prior to the beginning of the war. Specifically, the king's minister attempted to encourage Arjuna and his brothers to abandon their responsibilities and live according to the path of renunciation. The path of the renunciant was presented as higher and more worthy than the path of living an active life in society. Although the king was using these principles to justify not going to war, he was in fact, unwilling to follow these higher principles himself and to seek a higher standard in his own behavior. Arjuna, by contrast, seeks the highest ideal and is in doubt about his own training as a warrior and his duty as a householder.

Renunciants and householders observe differing codes of behavior. For example, a vow of poverty is a high ideal for a renunciant, but impractical for a householder. Restraining from all sexual intercourse is expected for a renunciant; a householder has one chosen partner. Control or management of one's energies and feelings are required by both codes of behavior, but the form of this restraint is different. Here the issue of how to manage one's action when confronted with evil-doers arises.

Krishna emphasizes that action that is performed in a desireless manner, without the hope or expectation of reward, is best. Therefore, in discriminating between right or wrong, a higher importance is given to the motive behind the action than to the form of the external action. For example, a person engaging in charitable work may be secretly seeking admiration and acknowledgement. A person may dress as a *sanyāsi* but crave money, power, or a sense of importance. For this reason, the *Bhagavad Gītā* advocates that behavior be judged not on appearance, but on the motive of the doer.

The Vedic seers were practical in their recommendation for how to live human life. They made a distinction between idealism and realism, and accepted realism as paramount. They defined non-violence as non-injury to others for one's personal gain, happiness, or comfort. They accepted the need to oppose evil forces and corruption. The logic behind this analysis is that a corrupt or evil person does not deserve pity but correction. A corrupt person tortures the weak and poorer members of society as long as he lives. These actions create strong impressions in him, leading to an extended hell-like suffering for his soul in subsequent lives. Stopping his actions not only frees the weak from torture, it also relieves the perpetrator. On the basis of this principle, moral punishment was prescribed for the establishment of a well-disciplined society.

Violence can be addressed with understanding, love, and patience, but sometimes it is necessary to counter the corrupt for the welfare of all. According to the *Dharmasāstra*,[4] a king is responsible for the sins of

---

[4] *Dharmasāstra* is a summary work pertaining to religious and legal duty. The *Dharmasāstra* derives its authority from the Vedas, though few, if any, of the

sinners if they are not properly restrained. This logic is the basis for Krishna directing Arjuna to fight. If one engages in fighting with the intention to protect society, then under the guiding principles of an active life, non-violence is sustained. But a *sanyāsi* has a different duty as prescribed in the *Manusmirti*, "Do not become angry in return towards one who has become angry towards you."[5]

The *Mahābhārata* itself presents these different positions. In one place, it states: "Do not become an evil-doer in dealing with evil-doers, but behave towards them like a saint. Enmity is not done away with enmity."[6] Arjuna cites this as one of the reasons he should not fight and kill. Yet elsewhere, Prahlādā, a seer and devotee, while discussing how a householder should behave says, "My friend, wise men have everywhere mentioned exceptions to the principle of forgiveness."[7] The teaching of the *Bhagavad Gītā* is about resolving this doubt and dilemma.

Tilak says, "The methods adopted by commentators of mixing up the mutually contradictory doctrines pertaining to the two paths of renunciation and Karma Yoga, without taking into account what dictum applies to which path, and how it is to be used give rise to a confusion regarding the true doctrine of Karma Yoga."

The philosophy of Karma Yoga is based on the foundation of the knowledge of the Supreme Self. One should realize the comprehensiveness of the *Ātman*, understanding and feeling that the individual soul is one with the soul of the whole universe. Accordingly, considering the whole universe as our family, we should regulate our activities, and that includes protecting society. Otherwise, society may be weakened or destroyed. The *Bhagavad Gītā* favors this engagement.

When I first began meditation I came across a slogan that has remained with me, "See the job, do the job, stay out of the misery." By following this injunctive, I discovered that there was always an action to be performed and that progress unfolded naturally with each step. The

---

contents can be directly linked with Vedic texts. The *Dharmasāstra* is important within the Hindu tradition as a source of religious law describing the life of an ideal householder and as a summation of principles regarding religion, law, and ethics.

[5] *Manusmirti* 6.48.
[6] *Mahābhārata Vana Parva* 206.44.
[7] *Mahābhārata Vana Parva* 28.8.

next step always presented itself. I honed my discrimination, learning to make appropriate choices. I trained my focus on the present moment and learned to trust the unfoldment. After many steps, I met my guru. His appearance in my life was part of the natural progression of my journey, though many steps still remained. My experience and understanding flourished under his guidance. Gradually, with his help, I found myself anchored in the all-pervasive present moment.

One day as we sat together, I complained about my responsibilities and the lack of time. "My boy, when you are able to sustain your realization while in the midst of the streets of Delhi, then you will be fully established in the Self," he said fondly. In this way he reminded me that the Self is always present, even during an onslaught of chaotic activity. We cannot remove ourselves from action. We dwell within a body and a world filled with activity. The Self is distinct from this activity, and always present. We can dwell in the Self and still be fully active in the world as we perform the responsibilities that present themselves to us. With his words of encouragement, my guru taught me the essence of the *Bhagavad Gītā*.

As the cycle of life continues, our own students now ask my wife and me, "Which *Bhagavad Gītā* should we read?" Although I believe the *Gītā Rahasya* is best, it remains daunting, perhaps too challenging for a new student of philosophy. And it is also out of print and hard to obtain. But since Tilak's insights remain worthy of deep study, I have provided the basic reasoning underlying his commentary, and will now offer a summary of the background from the *Mahābhārta* to help us understand how the circumstances of the civil war had come to pass. Within the verses of the *Bhagavad Gītā* I have avoided commentary, instead grouping verses with the intent of collating the specific topics Krishna presents to Arjuna. In order to orient the reader, each chapter begins with a summary. Although as a human being, I have a bias, I nonetheless hope to present the *Bhagavad Gītā* in a format whereby we can follow Tilak's example and "setting aside all criticisms and commentaries…independently and thoughtfully read the Gītā."

Background

The teaching of the *Bhagavad Gītā* is included within the epic known as the *Mahābhārta*. The story begins with an introduction to the lineage of the Kuru dynasty from which come the cousins of the Kaurava and the Pāndava families. King Dhritarāshtra is the head of the Kuru dynasty and the Kaurava family. The king, who is blind, has fathered 100 children; the eldest is Duryodhana.

The Pāndava lineage descends from Dhritarāshtra's younger brother Pāndu. Because of King Dhritarāshtra's blindness, Pāndu led the dynasty for a period of time, during which he strengthened and expanded the kingdom. After accomplishing this, he voluntarily relinquished royal life and handed responsibility for the kingdom back to Dhritarāshtra, who is aided by a third brother, Vidura. Pandu then retreated to a forest location with his two wives, Kunti and Madri. Kunti bore three children, Yudhisthira, Bhīma, and Arjuna, and Madri gave birth to a set of twins, Nakul and Sahadev.

Following the untimely death of their father, Pandu, their mothers bring the five brothers back to the capital city. There they are raised and trained alongside their Kaurava cousins. Bhīma, who is very strong, is often at odds with his cousin, Duryodhana. Arjuna is very skilled in archery and wins much praise from his teachers and elders. Duryodhana, insecure and jealous, develops an ever-increasing hatred towards his cousins, and becomes absorbed in fantasies of ways to remove them from his life. In time, aided by the vile advice of his maternal uncle, Shakuni, he develops a plan to get rid of the Pāndavas and secure the crown of the Kuru kingdom for himself.

The plotting takes a grave turn when King Dhritarāshtra accepts the will of the people and rightfully appoints his nephew Yudhisthira, the eldest Pandava cousin, as crown prince. This act, which opposes the personal ambitions of both Dhritarāshtra and Duryodhana, drives Duryodhana into a rage, and he enthusiastically agrees to initiate Shakuni's evil plot to murder Yudhisthira and his brothers. Fortunately for the Pāndavas, the plan is discovered by their paternal uncle Vidura, who assists in their escape. Duryodhana and the Kauravas are led to believe that the Pāndavas have been killed in a fire. Disguised as hermits, the five brothers hide in the forest for a period of years.

In due time, it is announced that an archery contest will be held to decide who will win the hand of Princess Draupadi. Arjuna enters the contest and wins. The special skill needed to win the contest exposes the identity of Arjuna, and the Kauravas come to know that the Pāndavas are still alive. When Dhritarāshtra receives the news, he invites the five brothers back to the kingdom.

Duryodhana had succeeded in becoming the crown prince during the absence of the Pāndavas. Upon their return, the issue of returning Yudhisthira's crown is raised. Dhritarāshtra leads the subsequent discussions and agrees to a partition of the kingdom to satisfy both crown princes. He retains the developed Hastināpura capital and surrounding area for himself and Duryodhana, and gives barren and hostile lands to the Pāndavas.

With the help of many supporters, the Pāndavas successfully develop this land and build a great and lavish city. This fuels Duryodhana's jealousy and rage once again. Shakuni presents yet another scheme to help Duryodhana rid himself of the Pāndavas. The five brothers are invited to the court in Hastināpura for a special gathering. There Shakuni, a master gambler in possession of a magical pair of dice, entices Yudhisthira to play a game of chance. Yudhisthira loses everything, including his brothers. Duryodhana then offers Yudhisthira a chance to win everything back if he offers Princess Draupadi as an offsetting bet. He loses again and the Pāndavas and Princess Draupadi become the property of Duryodhana.

Duryodhana's younger brother Dushasana now drags the princess into the royal court, pulling her by her hair, insulting her dignity and asserting that she, like the Pāndava brothers, is now a servant of the Kauravas. This indignity causes immense anguish for those who had trained and tutored the five brothers: the grandfather, Bhīsma, the archery teacher of the cousins, Dronacharya and other great warriors seated in the court. But all except the brother of the king, Vidura, remain silent. Vidura protests in defense of the Pandava brothers and the princess, but to no avail. Duryodhana then orders his brother to disrobe Draupadi before everyone. The elders and warriors in audience are shocked, but do not intervene. Dushasana tries to disrobe Draupadi, but as he pulls her sari, turning her body, the cloth is miraculously unending.

King Dhritarāshtra, realizing this humiliation could prompt a curse on his sons, intervenes and apologizes to Draupadi. He returns all of the winnings of the dice game back over to the Pāndava brothers, releasing them from the bondage of slavery.

Incensed at the loss of all he had won, Duryodhana threatens suicide and coerces his father to allow one last round of gambling. The terms of this round are that the loser be condemned to 12 years of exile into the forest, and a 13th year be spent incognito. If the identity of the loser is discovered during the 13th year, another cycle of 13 years would ensue. Obeying their uncle's orders, the Pāndavas play the round, and once again lose to Shakuni's cheating. And so the Pāndavas are exiled to the forest for 12 years. The 13th year is spent masquerading as peasants in the servitude of the royal family of Virata, the king of Matsya. Upon completion of the terms of the wager, the Pāndavas return and demand their kingdom be rightfully returned to them. But Duryodhana refuses.

A council of the supporters of the Pāndavas is held in Virata. Krishna opens the council by speaking of the rights of the Pāndavas and suggests that an emissary be sent to discuss possible solutions. Krishna's brother, Balarama[8], agrees on the need for further negotiations, yet emphasizes the folly of Yudhishthira. He claims that Yudhishthira lost himself in the excitement of gambling and thus foolishly lost his kingdom to Duryodhana. He falsely states that Yudhishthira was repeatedly dissuaded from playing, but would not listen, and that he was the one who initiated the challenge. "For this foolishness it is no use blaming Shakuni or Duryodhana," says Balarama. "Therefore the messenger should be humble when approaching the Kauravas to beg for a solution to avert war."

Satyaki, a powerful warrior and king in support of the Pāndavas, interrupts. "How can it be said that the Kauravas won the game by fair means? It was they who challenged him!" He goes on to explain how

---

[8] Balarama is Duryodhana's guru and favors him. When he later meets with Duryodhana he tells him how he spoke in his favor and chided his brother Krishna for taking the side of the Pāndavas. He then stated that he feels Krishna is not impartial.

Yudhishthira was not a skillful player, and how the *kṣatriya*[9] code of fearlessness and valor was used to the advantage of his opponents. They coerced him, thus forcing him to accept the challenge and play. In short, they won by cheating. If the Kauravas had been invited by Yudhishthira and his brothers to their home for a game of dice, and if they had then played and won the game, their winning could have been called fair. But the facts are different. The Kauravas *summoned* Yudhishthira to their capital. In that game he lost everything. "Surely this is not princely behavior on the part of Duryodhana!" Satyaki emphasizes.

He goes on to assert the brothers have acted righteously. "Even so, Yudhishthira and his brothers, has complied with all the conditions of the wager, living thirteen years in exile as promised. His father's kingdom is his due. Why should he not demand it, rather than ask humbly for something that is his right? Why should he demean himself out of fear that Duryodhana might become angry? He is already acting in anger. We know that Yudhishthira is not wrong, not one bit. He has most cruelly been wronged by his cousins.

"Duryodhana has been neither righteous nor honorable. He knows full well that the period of exile is over, and yet he is asserting that they failed at the very end of the thirteenth year. He claims they discovered Arjuna in an archery contest. And now they must go back into exile for another twelve years! This is not righteous according to our code. His uncle, Vidura, has repeatedly advised Duryodhana not to be so cruel. He asked him to return their kingdom, but Duryodhana remains entrenched in his hatred."

The meeting closed with the decision to send a messenger to the court and continue negotiations. After hearing the proposal of the Pāndavas to avert the war, Dhritarāshtra tells him he will need to consult with his court before arriving at a decision. He tells the messenger he will send his response via his ambassador, Sañjaya.

His minister, Sañjaya, soon delivered Dhritarāshtra's response. "I send my best wishes to my sons Yudhishthira, Bhīma, Arjuna, Nakula and Sahadeva and also to my dear Krishna and others gathered. My dear Yudhishthira, I request you be for peace. You are full of good qualities.

---

[9] *Kṣatriya* is the second highest in the social class or Hindu caste system. It is the ruling and military class, with responsibilities for leadership and protection of society.

You are known for your gentleness, your love of steadiness, and hatred of all crookedness. You have been born into a great family. A base deed should not be considered by you, who are so high-minded. If, after all these years of righteousness, you choose now to do a shameful deed, it will most certainly spoil your good name. I hope you will not do a thing that will cause the destruction of this world. It is a sin that will lead you to hell. Whether you win or lose is of minor importance.

"There is nothing like the sacrifice of one's life for the sake of family," the messenger for Dhritarāshtra continued, "Indeed, they alone will be blessed, who instead of destroying their cousins, give up their lives for the sake of family. If you insist on fighting, you may be able to destroy them. But what will you achieve? You will be unhappy for all your life, as the death of one's relations does not give happiness. Yours will be a living death if you survive after the death of your cousins.

"You must think twice before you decide for war. I feel that nothing good can come of either victory or defeat. I pray this calamity may be averted. I have hopes that Krishna and Arjuna will not disregard these words of mine. I am speaking for the welfare of the world. Krishna and Arjuna will die before they ever think of disobeying me."

Yudhishthira was amazed and deeply distressed by the words of his uncle. In anger he told the ambassador Sañjaya of the unfairness of his uncle's attempt to accuse him of deliberate cruelty. Of course he wants peace, and has been against this war from the start, making numerous attempts to settle the matter. "Who would want war when it is possible to avert it with compromise? What cursed fool would choose to fight if he could get what he wanted without having to fight for it?

"I have realized one thing. Fire, when it is fed, is not quenched. It is never satisfied. Its appetite grows with what it feeds upon. The mind of Dhritarāshtra is like fire. The more he has, the more he wants. If it had not been for this greed, we would never have had to wander in the forest like mendicants. He seeks protection in the nobleness of others, being bereft of that quality himself. He has been guilty of certain acts towards us. Let him now be prepared for retaliation. The king commands great wealth. Why does he weep and moan? He encourages his son Duryodhana's crooked ways. He has aided and abetted his cruelty. He thinks of only one thing, the pleasure of his son, a son steeped in sin, who is too proud, arrogant and haughty to know how to behave towards his elders. His vile language does not befit a son of the most ancient family on the earth. And, for such a son, your king, knowing and willingly abandons what is right.

"Dhritarāshtra wants the entire earth. He wants his sovereignty to be undisputed. How can that be possible when he has taken the kingdom by deception and clutches it like a child clings to a toy snatched from the hands of another? Tell him we only seek fairness. Tell him to return my lands and there will be no war."

Sañjaya replies, "You have not heard the message completely. The king says, 'Consider the life of man on this earth. It is short. Why should you let it end in infamy?' A life of shame is a life lost. The Kauravas may not give up your kingdom without a war. Even if you prevail, it will be better to spend the rest of your life begging for alms in another kingdom. That would be nobler than gaining sovereignty over the entire world. You have spent many years in the company of men who have renounced the world. Why, then, do you still desire things of the world? All those years of righteousness will go to waste if you persist in this sin. Concentrate instead on the acquisition of wealth for the next world and abandon all claims to this world. What could you possibly achieve by winning this war? All your glory will be eclipsed because of this action of yours. Desist from this!"

Krishna then replies to Sañjaya, "My first concern is for the welfare of the Pāndavas. I do not at all understand the message of the king. Why does he attribute all the sins to his poor nephew, knowing full well where the blame has to be laid? Yudhishthira could have killed his Kaurava cousins long ago. We asked him to do so. But he thought that it would not be right. And for that the king blames him! Has the king lost his sense because of his extreme worry about his sons? You are well aware of the duty of a *ksatriya*. A *ksatriya* should restrain the breaker of law. This king has no right to talk about what is right and wrong.

"We are for peace. We do not want the whole world to die because of the obstinate pride of one man. It pains us to see so many people suffer because one man is so unyielding, and his father so greedy. We want the world to live and the people to be happy and protected. This is our responsibility. Please go and tell your king that I will come to his court. I will do my best to convince that foolish Duryodhana that he should do what is right by the Pāndavas."

Sañjaya returns to Hastināpura and relates what has happened. After some time Krishna arrives. Discussions take place without success. Finally, for the sake of peace, and to avert a disastrous war, Krishna proposes that the Pāndavas be given only five villages to satisfy their claim. Duryodhana vehemently refuses, saying he will not part with even that land which would fit into the eye of a needle. Thus, the stage has been set for war. As the two sets of cousins with their allies are staged on a battlefield, the story continues with Arjuna's mental collapse and Krishna's teaching, known as the *Bhagavad Gītā*.

Chapter I
Despondency of Arjuna

The *Bhagavad Gītā* consists of eighteen chapters. The first chapter, which is prefatory, introduces the participants, and presents Arjuna's quandary and the primary question that he addresses to Lord Krishna. The core of Krishna's teaching is contained in chapters two and three and then expanded upon in the subsequent chapters.

Another commentator of the *Bhagavad Gītā*[10], Shripad Damodar Satwalekar (1867-1968), sheds light on the first chapter. He illuminates Arjuna's despondency with his analysis of the diplomatic ploys used by Sañjaya on behalf of Dhritarāshtra. According to Satwalekar, "This last attempt of the Kauravas to dissuade the Pāndavas from going to war by preaching religious sermons is indicative of the crooked Machiavellian diplomacy of the Imperialist." Knowing that the Pāndavas are, by instinct, righteous, Dhritarāshtra hopes to use religious principles to weaken their resolve by shifting the responsibility for the war onto them. The impact and success of that diplomacy is seen in Arjuna's collapse of resolve. At a critical moment, Arjuna, strongly affected by these sermons, collapses into a fit of dejection; the world conqueror, now indifferent towards the world, is ready to retire to the forest as a mendicant.

In the first chapter of the *Gītā*, Arjuna restates the arguments Sañjaya had posited as reasons the Pāndavas should not fight. He questions whether one who protects himself against an oppressor might not be committing the same sin as the oppressor. In essence, he wonders whether his action would be sinful. If he behaves in the same manner as those who are overcome by greed, is not his behavior also reprehensible? Arjuna has been trained as a warrior, but now he is unsure whether he has a right to fight against evil.

---

[10] *Shrimad Bhagawad-Gītā*, Part 1-3, Pundit Shripad Damodar Satwalekar, Swādhyāya Mandal, Anandashram, Pardi.

Swami Bawra taught that every action has three parts: *karma* is the motive behind an action, the action itself is *kriyā*, and the doer is *karta*. Arjuna asks whether his motive will affect the results of his action. He is worried that his actions might lead to his downfall and jeopardize his afterlife. To respond to this question, let us consider the example of two different people who each cut into a stomach with a knife. A thief may cut a person in order to steal their money. But a surgeon who cuts a person does so to save their life. The *Gītā* teaches that the result of an action depends upon the motive behind the action and not the action itself.

Slokas

Dhritārashtra said: (1) O Sañjaya, what did my sons and the sons of Pāndu, desirous of war, do when they assembled together, on the sacred field of Kuruksetra?

Sañjaya said: (2) Prince Duryodhana, seeing the Pāndava army in battle-array, approached his teacher, Drona, and said, (3) O teacher, behold this mighty army of the Pāndavas, arrayed by the son of Drupada, your wise disciple. (4) There are heroes, mighty bowmen, the equals of Bhīma and Arjuna; Yuydhāna, Virāta and Drupada, (5) and Dhrstaketu, Cekitāna, and the valiant king of Kāsi, Purujit, and Kuntibhoja, and that eminent man named Śaibya, (6) as also the heroic Yudhāmanya, and the valiant Uttamaujā, and the son of Subhadrā and the sons of Draupadī, all mighty warriors.

(7) O best of the twice-born, know also the names of the most distinguished on our side, who are the leaders of my army. I name them for your information. (8) Yourself, Bhīsma and Karna, the victorious Kripa, Aśvatthāmā, Vikarna and Bhurisravā, the son of Somadatta; (9) And many other heroes also, who are determined to lay down their lives for me. They are experts in various weapons and well-skilled in battle. (10) This army of ours which is protected by Bhīsma is unlimited, whereas their army is limited. (11) Therefore, all respectively stand in your assigned positions and protect Bhīsma on all sides.

(12) Then the oldest of the Kauravas, Bhīsma, roared like a lion and blew his conch to cheer Duryodhana. (13) Then, conches, kettle-drums, tabors, drums, cow horns suddenly blared forth. And the sound was tumultuous. (14) Then Śri Krishna and Arjuna, stationed in their chariot yoked with white horses, blew their divine conches. (15) Śri Krishna blew

his conch, Pāñcajanya, Arjuna his Devadatta and Bhīma his great conch Paundra. (16) King Yudhisthira, the son of Kunti, blew his conch Anantavijaya and Nakula and Sahadeva blew their conches Sughosa and Manipuspaka. (17) Similarly, Kāsirāja, the supreme bowman, Śikandī, the might warrior, Dhristadyumna and Virāta, and Sātyaki the invincible; (18) Drupada and the sons of Draupadī, and the strong-armed son of Subhadrā, all blew their conches. (19) And that tumultuous uproar, which shook the earth and the firmament, rent the hearts of Dhritarāshtra's sons. (20) Then, seeing that the Kauravas were properly arrayed, and when the attack by weapons was about to start, Arjuna, who had Hanumān as his banner crest, took up his bow and spoke to Śri Krishna,

Arjuna said: (21) Place my chariot, O Krishna, between the two armies (22) that I may observe those standing here prepared to engage in battle. Let me see with whom I have to fight in this war, and (23) gaze on those fighters who have collected here with the intention of helping the cause of the evil-minded Duryodhana.

Sañjaya said: (24) O Dhritarāshtra, when Arjuna spoke thus to Śri Krishna, he drove and placed the splendid chariot of Arjuna between the two armies, and (25) he said in the presence of Bhīsma and Drona, and all other kings, O Arjuna, look at these Kauravas assembled here.

(26) Then Arjuna saw all who were assembled were his own elders, ancestors, preceptors, maternal uncles, brothers, sons, grandsons, and friends, (27) and fathers-in-law, and dear ones in both armies. When he had seen that all who had assembled there were kinsman, Arjuna, the son of Kunti, being filled with intense compassion and despair said these words,

Arjuna said: (28-30) O Krishna, seeing these, my kinsmen, assembled here eager to fight, my limbs fail me, my mouth is parched, my body trembles and my hair stands on end, the bow, Godiva, slips from my hand, and my skin is burning. I can no longer stand upright, and my mind is in a whirl. (31) O Keshava, I see adverse omens and do not perceive any good will come from killing my kinsmen in the battle. (32) O Krishna, I have no desire for victory, for sovereignty, or for pleasures. O Govinda, of what use is having sovereignty or enjoyment or life itself to us? (33) Those for whose sake we desire kingdom, enjoyments and pleasures are standing here for battle renouncing life and wealth. (34-35) Teachers, fathers, sons and also grandfathers, uncles, fathers-in-law and grandsons, brothers-in-law and other relatives have all risen to kill us, yet I do not wish to kill them O Madhusūdana, even for obtaining the kingdom of the three worlds, and even less for this earth.

(36) O Janārdana, what pleasure may be ours by killing these Kauravas? Although they are felons, yet by killing them sin will attach to us. (37) Therefore, it is not proper that we ourselves should kill the Kauravas, who are our kinsmen. For how, O Mādhava, can we become happy by killing our own kinsmen? (38-39) Though they, whose minds are overpowered by greed, see no evil in the destruction of a clan and no sin in treachery to friends, why, O Krishna, should we not learn to shun this crime—we who see the evil of ruining a clan?

(40) With the ruin of a clan, its ancient traditions are perished, and when traditions perish, lawlessness overtakes the whole clan. (41) When lawlessness prevails, O Krishna, the women of the family become corrupt; and when anything adverse happens to our women, the whole society suffers. (42) This social disintegration leads to hell for the clan itself and its destroyers; and the spirit of their ancestors fall degraded, deprived of the ritual offerings. (43) By these misdeeds of destroying the clan confusion reigns in society, class and caste, and the ancient traditions of the clan and class are destroyed. (44) We have heard that person whose family rites are abolished, must necessarily reside in hell.

(45) Alas, we are engaged in committing a great sin in that we have risen to kill our own kinsmen out of greed for the pleasures of sovereignty. (46) If the well-armed sons of Dhritarāshtra should slay me in battle, unresisting and unarmed, that will be better for me. (47) Having spoken thus on the battlefield, Arjuna, whose mind was agitated by grief, cast aside his bow and arrows and sat down on his seat in the chariot.

Chapter II
Sāmkhya and Yoga

Arjuna shares his reasoning and doubts with Krishna and then falls quiet in surrender to his friend and mentor. He is ready to listen. If Arjuna's reasons for not fulfilling his responsibility had been correct, Krishna would have agreed with him. The story would have ended. Krishna would have turned to Arjuna and affirmed his analysis, saying, "Excellent Arjuna, let's discard our weapons and leave the battlefield, retiring to the forest as mendicants so the Kauravas can rule as they wish." But instead Krishna's teaching continues for seventeen chapters.

The *Mahābhārata* has presented the Pāndavas as victims of the ruling power, the Kauravas. Krishna and Arjuna are both members of the *kṣatriya* class with responsibility for ruling and protecting society. Protection includes providing an umbrella of safety so that society may prosper without fear. But Arjuna, a skilled, powerful and famed *kṣatriya*, is now faced with opponents who are family, friends and teachers. The ideas skillfully planted by Sañjaya on behalf of Dhritarāshtra have now blossomed into full blown doubts in Arjuna's mind, doubts that have overcome his reason.

Krishna's teaching is a teaching of empowerment. This is a message from a heroic teacher to a heroic pupil. It provides the practical application of the spiritual knowledge of the Upanishads in everyday life. Because Arjuna has presented his doubts according to the logic of a renunciant, Krishna begins to correct his understanding by clarifying important points held by those who follow an analytical path of knowledge called Sāmkhya. Sāmkhya has traditionally espoused the renunciation of action. It was from this teaching that Dhritarāshtra drew the arguments intended to dissuade the Pāndavas from going to war.

According to the path of knowledge, here called Sāmkhya, the soul or indwelling Self is distinctly different from the physical body, and this indweller is the real person, not the body. The soul and the body each have specific qualities, and the qualities of one do not belong or can never be attained by the other. One is real, unchanging and indestructible and the other is unreal, ever changing and destructible.

Krishna then goes on to address the *kṣatriya* code and the responsibilities of one belonging to this class. Finally he introduces his teaching on Yoga, which includes skill and equanimity in action.

Slokas

Sañjaya said: (1) To him, who was thus overcome with pity, whose eyes were filled with tears, who was sorrow-stricken and who was dejected, Śri Krishna spoke these words:

Śri Krishna said: (2) O Arjuna, how has this infamous conduct entered your mind in this time of crisis. It is unfit for a noble person. It is disgraceful and leads to hell. (3) Yield not to unmanliness, O Arjuna, it does not become you. Cast off this base weakness of heart and stand up, O scorcher of foes.

Arjuna said: (4) O Destroyer of enemies, how shall I aim arrows in battle against Bhīsma and Drona who are worthy of reverence? (5) It is better even to live in this world by begging rather than slay these most venerable teachers. If I should slay my teachers, though they are degraded by desire for wealth, I would be enjoying only blood-stained pleasures here. (6) I do not know which will be better for us—whether we should vanquish them or they should vanquish us. Even though these Kauravas stand in battle array against us we will not wish to live after slaying them. (7) On account of my natural temperament being weakened by adverse circumstances, my mind is in doubt as to my duty. I request you to tell me what is good for me. I am your disciple, instruct me, who has surrendered to you. (8) Even though I might win a prosperous kingdom on the earth free from foes, or even the sovereignty of heaven I do not see how this will dispel the grief that is drying up my senses.

Sañjaya said: (9) Having spoken thus to Śri Krishna, Arjuna, the slayer of foes, said, 'I shall not fight' and became silent. (10) Then, Śri Krishna, smiling, spoke these words to Arjuna, who was sitting dejected between the two armies.

Śri Krishna said: (11) You grieve for those who should not be grieved for; yet you speak about knowledge. The even-minded grieve neither for the living nor the dead. (12) There never was a time when I did not exist, or you, or any of these kings of men; nor will there be a time in the future when all of us shall cease to be. (13) Just as the Self associated with a body passes through childhood, youth and old age, so to at death it passes into another body. The wise one is not deluded about this.

(14) O son of Kunti, the contact of the senses with their objects gives rise to feelings of cold and heat, of pleasure and pain. They come and go, never lasting long. Endure them, O Arjuna. (15) It is the steadfast person alone, O preeminent among men, who remains balanced towards pleausre and pain, is not swayed by them, and thus becomes capable of attaining immortality.

(16) That which is not (unreal) cannot be as if it is; and that which is (real) cannot be as if it is not; in this way the seers of truth have perceived the truth about the real and unreal. (17) Know That to be indestructible by which all this is pervaded. None can cause the destruction of this imperishable. (18) These bodies inhabited by the eternal, indestructible and immeasurable embodied Self are said to be perishable. Therefore, fight O Arjuna.

(19) He who considers the *atman* (embodied Self) as the slayer or he who considers that it is slain are both wrong. For the *atman* neither slays nor is slain. (20) This Self is never born, nor does it ever die; having come into existence, it will never cease to be; it is unborn, eternal, unchanging and primeval; it is not slain when the body is slain. (21) Whosoever knows it to be indestructible, eternal, unborn, and imperishable—how and whom, O Arjuna, can he cause it to be killed, and whom does he kill? (22) Just as a man, casts off worn out clothes and puts on others that are new, so does the embodied Self cast off worn out bodies and enter into others that are new. (23) Weapons do not cut it; fire does not burn it; water does not wet it, and wind does not wither it. (24) It cannot be cleft; it cannot be burnt; it cannot be wetted and it cannot be withered. It is permanent, all-pervading, stable, immovable and eternal. (25) This Self is said to be imperceptible (not perceptible by the organs), inconceivable (impossible of being understood), and immutable. Therefore, knowing this to be such, it is not proper that you should grieve.

(26) Or, even if you think this Self is constantly born and constantly dies, even then, O might-armed one, it does not become you to feel grief. (27) Because to one that is born, death is certain, and to one that dies, birth is certain; therefore, about an unavoidable matter, you ought not to

grieve. (28) All created beings are imperceptible in the beginning, perceptible in the middle, and imperceptible at the end. What is there to grieve over all of this?

(29) Some look upon this as a wonder, others speak of it as a wonder; still another hears of it as a wonder, but even after hearing of it, no one knows it really. (30) This embodied Self is eternal and indestructible, O Arjuna; therefore, it is not fit for you to grieve for any being.

(31) Besides, even if you consider your own duty, it does not befit you to waver. For, to a *ksatriya*, there is no greater good than a righteous war. (32) O Arjuna, this war, which is indeed a door to heaven, found open without effort, falls only to those *ksatriyas* who are fortunate. (33) But, if you will not carry on this righteous warfare, then you will have abandoned your duty and lost your honor, and incurred sin. (34) Further, people will speak ill of you for all time, and for one who has been honored, dishonor is worse than death. (35) The great warriors will think that you withdrew from battle on account of fear. These men who held you in high esteem will speak lightly of you now. (36) Your enemies, slandering your prowess, will use words, which should never be uttered. What could be more painful than that? (37) If slain you shall win heaven, or if victorious you will enjoy the earth; therefore, arise, O Arjuna, determined on battle. (38) Looking upon pleasure and pain, gain and loss, victory and defeat as alike, start the battle; acting thus you will not incur sin.

(39) This knowledge stated to you is according to Sāmkhya. Now listen to this with regard to Yoga, by following which you break through the bonds of *karma* (action). (40) Here, there is no loss of effort, nor is there any harm. Even a little of this practice protects one from great danger.

(41) O Arjuna, on this path the intellect, which discerns between the doable and non-doable, must be one-pointed; the thoughts and desires of the irresolute are many branched and endless. (42) The unwise rejoice in the words of the Vedas and utter flowery speeches, saying that nothing else is of importance. (43) They are full of worldly desires, intent on gaining heaven and offer rebirth as the fruit of works. They look upon the Vedas as consisting entirely of various rites and prescribe specific actions for the attainment of pleasure and power. (44) Those who seek pleasure and power are enamored by that speech; thereby their intellects are unable to develop a concentrated state and resolute insight.

(45) O Arjuna, the Vedas deal with the three *gunas* (attributes of nature). Be free from these attributes and indifferent towards the pairs of opposites. Without clinging to selfish interests, become established in the Self. (46) What use does a thirsty person have for a water reservoir when all sides of it are flooded? In the same way, what necessity do the Vedas have for a person who knows the Self?

(47) Your authority extends only to the performance of action; obtaining or not obtaining the fruit is never within your control; therefore, do not be one who performs action with a motive that a specific fruit should be obtained; nor insist on not-performing action.

(48) Abandoning attachment and established in Yoga, perform action with an even mind towards success or failure. Evenness of mind is known as Yoga. (49) For, action with attachment is far inferior to action with reason. Seek refuge in this equability of reason. Miserable are they who act with a motive for results. (50) A person who is established in equable reason remains untouched by sin or merit in this world; therefore, take shelter in Yoga. The skill in performing action is known as Yoga.

(51) The wise, possessed of this evenness of mind, having abandoned the fruit of action, are freed from the bondage of rebirth, and reach the state that is beyond all pain. (52) When your intellect has crossed beyond the tangle of delusion; you will become indifferent towards whatever you have heard or have yet to hear. (53) When your intellect, currently confused by the conflict of opinions, will become fixed and immovable in the Self, then you will attain this Yoga.

Arjuna said: (54) O Krishna, what is the description of a person of stable wisdom? How does he speak? How does he sit? How does he walk?

Śri Krishna said: (55) When a man abandons all desires of the mind, and is satisfied in the Self, alone by the Self, then he is said to be one of steady wisdom. (56) He, whose mind is not agitated by adversity, who is not longing for pleasures, and from whom attachment, fear and anger have departed, is called a sage of steady wisdom. (57) His reason is said to be steady whose mind is without attachment in all things, and who feels no exaltation or aversion regarding the agreeable or disagreeable which befalls him. (58) When a person draws his senses from the objects of sense as the tortoise draws in its limbs from all sides, then his wisdom stands firm.

(59) The objects of senses leave the abstinent dweller, yet the relish in them does not leave until the Supreme Self is realized. (60) These turbulent senses forcibly carry away the mind of even the wise person who is striving to control them, Arjuna. (61) So, having restrained these senses, he should remain fixed on Me as the Supreme. For his wisdom is steady whose senses are under his control.

(62) To a person thinking about sense-objects, there arises attachment to them; from attachment arises desire to possess them, from an obstacle to that possession arises anger; (63) from anger there arises delusion; from delusion the loss of memory; from the loss of memory the destruction of discrimination; and with the destruction of discrimination, he is lost and perishes. (64) But he, who is disciplined and established in the Self, moves among the objects of the senses free from attraction and aversion, and attains tranquility. (65) In serenity unhappiness is destroyed, for the intellect at once becomes steady for the tranquil-minded.

(66) There is no wisdom for the unsteady, nor is there establishment in the Self. For one who is not established in the Self, there can be no tranquility, and how can one who is lacking peace have happiness? (67) The mind that follows the senses experiencing their objects enslaves the reason of the person, just as the wind carries away a boat in the water. (68) Therefore, O Arjuna, the reason is said to be steady in that person whose senses are controlled on all sides from the objects of the senses.

(69) The controlled one is awake in that which is night for everyone else; and such a sage looks upon that as night in which every other living being is awake. (70) Just as all waters enter the full and undisturbed ocean, though it is being filled on all sides, so does tranquility remain in the person in whom all objects of the senses enter without disturbing his state of well-being, not by the one who desires and craves for the objects of the senses.

(71) He alone acquires tranquility who performs action having given up all desire, abiding without longing and possession and the sense of mine-ness and egoism. (72) O Arjuna, this is called the *Brāhmic-state* (eternal state); having attained this, the man does not remain in ignorance; and established in this state even at the end of life, he attains oneness with *Brāhman*.

Chapter III
Yoga of Action

Arjuna wants clarification. He is confused because he thinks that Krishna is praising knowledge as superior to action, and at the same time, praising action as superior to knowledge. Arjuna's thinking is rooted in the prevalent ideas of his era: If an aspirant pursues knowledge alone, he leaves society and becomes a renunciant. On the other hand, a person choosing a life of action must live according to the wisdom established in social rules of conduct. Here Krishna extols wisdom and knowledge as a great path, while also advocating action and duty, which Arjuna finds inconsistent.

Krishna responds to Arjuna by clarifying that while there are indeed two paths, abstention from action is not the criteria for becoming free. Action is inescapable; it pervades our bodies and the world. The key is to learn to participate without attachment. Proper discrimination is necessary no matter what lifestyle is chosen. Krishna goes so far as to say that the path of action is *superior* to inaction. We must perform the duties related to our circumstances and status, but without the expectation of specific results.

Krishna explains to Arjuna that when an individual gains realization and becomes established in the Self, their work should continue. Abandonment of society is not advised. He gives examples of great men who have become realized and continue to perform action. He himself has no personal needs but continues to act for the welfare of the world. Society is uplifted by those who, having attained a higher state, continue to teach and act for the benefit of others.

Krishna describes how all action takes place in nature, *prakriti*, and is governed by its attributes or qualities. The Self or soul is separate from this activity, yet as a result of egoism, we believe incorrectly that we are the actor and doer. Krishna explains how this egoistic tendency arises out of the quality of *rajas*, one of the attributes of nature. Once this egoistic

31

self is accepted as our real Self, we feel a loss, become prompted by desire to overcome the loss, and consequently feel anger if that desire is thwarted. This cycle of misery envelops the soul, which leads to a loss of discrimination. Krishna then reminds Arjuna once again that the soul is truly above all the unfoldment and activity of nature.

Slokas

Arjuna said: (1) O Krishna, if you consider that knowledge is superior to action, then why are you engaging me in this terrible action? (2) By this seemingly mixed advice you are confusing my understanding. Therefore, tell me definitely only that thing by which I shall attain the highest good.

Śri Krishna said: (3) O sinless one, as I indicated, in this world the path is of two kinds: the path of knowledge of the Sāmkhyas and the path of action of the Yogins. (4) Not by abstaining from action does a person attain the highest state; nor does one attain perfection by merely renouncing action. (5) It is impossible to live without performing action. We are forced into action, even against our will, by the attributes that are inherent in material nature. (6) He who merely controls the organs of action, but continually dwells on the objects of the senses, is called a hypocrite. (7) But the person who controls his senses by means of the intellect, and, without attachment, engages the organs of action in the Yoga of action, is superior, O Arjuna. (8) Perform the action according to your skills and abilities; it is better to perform action than to avoid action. Even the maintenance of the body requires action.

(9) Aside from action for the purpose of sacrifice, this world is bound by action; perform work for this purpose Arjuna, free from attachment and the expectation of fruit. (10) In the beginning, the Lord of all beings created living beings together with sacrifice and said; "By means of this sacrifice may you grow and fulfill your desires." (11) By this process, please the gods and the gods will support you. Thus nourishing one another, you may obtain the highest good. (12) The gods, being satisfied by sacrifice, will bestow on you the enjoyments you desire. He who enjoys the bounty of the gods without acknowledgement and participating is a thief. (13) Those good men who partake of what remains after the performance of sacrifice are released from all sin. The wicked, who cook only for their own sake, eat only sin. (14) Living beings come into

existence from food; food results from rain; rain results from sacrifice; and sacrifice is made possible by action. (15) Know that the origin of action is from knowledge, and that all of this knowledge has sprung out of the Supreme Self; therefore, the all-pervading One is eternally present in sacrifice.

(16) The person who does not support the cycle set in motion lives in sin satisfying the senses, his life is lived in vain. (17) But for the person who rejoices in the Self, who is satisfied with the Self, and who is content in the Self alone, nothing remains to be accomplished. (18) He has nothing to gain whether by doing or not doing; and there is no selfish purpose of his own which is mixed up with all created beings. (19) Therefore, without attachment do your work which ought to be done. For a person who works without attachment attains the Supreme.

(20) Janaka and others thus attained release by performing action. In the same way, it is proper that you should perform action, keeping an eye to universal welfare. (21) Whatever a great man does, other men also will do. Whichever standard he sets, the world follows. (22) For Me, Arjuna, there is nothing in all the three worlds which ought to be done, nor is there anything not acquired that ought to be acquired. Yet I go on working. (23) If I did not continue to work unwearied, O Arjuna, men would follow My path. (24) If I do not do work, these men would be lost; and I will be causing chaos in life and thereby ruining all those people. (25) Just as the ignorant, attached to their work, act, O Arjuna, so too the learned should act without any attachment for the welfare of the world. (26) The man of knowledge should not unsettle the faith of the ignorant attached to action, but should himself become a performer of action and make others perform willingly.

(27) All actions take place as a result of the attributes of nature, *prakriti*. Those deluded by egoism think, "I am the doer." (28) But, Arjuna, he who knows the truth about the divisions of the attributes and their functions, knows that the attributes as senses merely abide with the attributes as sense-objects, and is not attached. (29) Those who are deluded by the attributes become attached to the attributes and actions. But he who knows the truth should not unsettle the ignorant who do not know. (30) For this reason, surrendering all your actions to Me, with a mind fixed on the Self, giving up expectation and mine-ness, fight, without any mental disturbance.

(31-32) Those devout persons, who act according to this advice, without finding fault with it, they too become free from the bonds of action, but know that those, who do not act according to this teaching, finding fault with it, senseless and devoid of all knowledge are therefore lost. (33) Even the realized soul acts according to their inherent nature; all beings follow their nature. What will repression do? (34) Each sense has fixed attachment to and aversion for its corresponding object. One should not become subject to this affection and repulsion, because they are enemies of men. (35) Better one's own duty, though deficient, than the duty of another well-performed. Better is death in one's own duty; the duty of another invites danger.

Arjuna said: (36) Then impelled by what inspiration does a man commit sin, as if coerced, but not desiring it?

Śri Krishna said: (37) Know that in this matter, the enemy is desire, which is most greedy and most sinful, born out of the attribute of *rajas*; and out of anger; (38) just as fire is covered by smoke or a mirror by dust, or as the embryo is encased in the membrane, so is this world enveloped by desire. (39) That, which is an insatiable fire, that constant enemy of the intelligent Self in the shape of desire, envelops all knowledge and is difficult to gratify.

(40) The senses, mind and intellect are said to be the house of it; by the support of these, it puts aside knowledge and throws the man into confusion. (41) Therefore, O Arjuna, first control the senses and destroy this sinful thing which destroys knowledge and discrimination. (42) The senses are higher; the mind is beyond the senses; the intellect is higher than the mind; and it (*ātman*) is beyond the reason. (43) O Arjuna, thus realizing that which is beyond the intellect, control the mind with the help of the intellect and destroy this enemy, which is difficult to conquer in the shape of desire.

Chapter IV
Renunciation of Action in Knowledge

Krishna begins by explaining to Arjuna that this ancient teaching was first given to the Sun god. In other words, as astrophysics would indicate, it dates from the birth of our solar system. This is an indication that pure knowledge is never absent from the development of matter. Moreover, this knowledge was instilled in the first humans, Manu and his son. Therefore, knowledge—the quality of Self—is ever present within all beings.

Knowledge becomes overshadowed or lost as a result of humankind's external focus. Krishna tells Arjuna he has now presented this special teaching to him. Beginning in the middle of the second chapter and through the third chapter Krishna has taught the essence of Yoga. The balance of the *Gītā* will fortify this teaching and provide a structure for Arjuna's learning.

The Sanskrit title of this chapter is *jñāna-karma-sannyāsa*. Krishna has advised and will continue to advise that one is to give up motive, desire and expectation while continuing to act with the guidance of reason and discrimination. Tilak emphasizes that this *karma-sannyāsa* is not to be confused with *karma-tyāga*, which means to abandon action. So, renunciation according to Krishna requires relinquishing the fruit of an action, and not the action itself.

Krishna then answers Arjuna, who is baffled by Krishna's claim to have taught this Yoga at the beginning of time. He explains that the Self remains unborn, unchanging, as His active, divine power takes form and acts for the protection of righteousness. Likewise, His life sets an example for how we can remain internally connected even as nature works through our body, senses, mind, ego and intellect. With proper knowledge we can be active, yet remain unattached as a renunciate of action. Then Krishna clarifies for Arjuna the meaning of action, of wrong action, and of inaction. He emphasizes that one can be established or inactive internally

35

in the midst of external action. Such a person is not bound by action. In contrast, a person may attempt to remain inactive, but, because the mind is disturbed with attachments born of desire, fear and anxiety, he remains active internally.

Our focus, which can be called our worship, determines the results of our activity. We should expect nothing different. In other words, we should not expect to attain a state of continuous happiness by desiring material objects, which produce only transitory pleasures. Our ignorance can only bring sorrow. In the end, Krishna advises that the pursuit of knowledge is superior to all other sacrifices and that supreme peace is attained when one has gained the pure knowledge of the Self.

Slokas

Śri Krishna continues: (1) I taught this imperishable Yoga to Vivasvāt (Sun god); Vivasvāt taught it to Manu (first man); and Manu declared it to Iksvāku (his son). (2) Thus handed down in succession, the royal sages knew this Yoga, but after the lapse of time this Yoga no longer exists on this earth, O Arjuna. (3) The same ancient Yoga has been taught by Me to you today, as you are My devotee and friend. It is the supreme mystery.

Arjuna said: (4) Your birth was later and that of Vivasvāt was much earlier. How then am I to understand that you taught it in the beginning?

Śri Krishna said: (5) O Arjuna, both you and I have lived through many lives. I know all this, but you do not know them. Though I am unborn, imperishable, and the Lord of all beings, yet by governing My own nature (*prakriti*) I am born by My own power (*māyā*). (7) O Arjuna, whenever righteousness declines and unrighteousness rises, I manifest Myself. (8) I take birth in different ages for protecting the good, destroying the wicked, and for establishing right action once again.

(9) He who knows the truth underlying My divine births and actions is not born again after leaving the body; he comes to Me, Arjuna. (10) Free from passion, fear and anger, absorbed in me, taking refuge in Me, purified by the fire of knowledge, many have attained My being.

(11) In whatever way men and women worship Me, I reward them accordingly. (It is) the path laid down by Me, Arjuna, that people tread in different ways. (12) They, who desire the fruits of their actions, sacrifice

here to deities; because success, resulting from action, is quickly attained in this world.

(13) The system of four castes was created by Me according to the distinction of qualities and actions. Though I am their creator, know me as non-doer and immutable. (14) Actions do not taint Me, nor have I a desire for the fruits of actions. He who knows Me thus is not bound by actions. (15) Knowing this, the ancient seekers after emancipation performed action; therefore, do you also perform action as it was performed by ancients in the past.

(16) Even the wise are confused as to what is action and what is inaction. I shall explain to you that kind of action, knowing which; you will be released from wrongdoing. (17) One must understand the nature of action, the nature of wrong action, and also the nature of inaction. It is difficult to understand the ways of action. (18) One who sees inaction in action, and action in inaction is wise among humans; he is established within the Self and performs all actions.

(19) He, whose undertakings are devoid of desire and motive, whose actions are burnt by the fire of knowledge, is considered a learned man by the wise. (20) He, having abandoned the attachment for the fruits of action, ever content, depending on nothing, even when performing action, in effect does nothing at all. (21) Free from expectation and attachment, with intellect and mind controlled, and performing work with the body, he incurs no sin. (22) Content with what comes to him, free from the pairs of opposites, devoid of jealousy, even-minded in success and failure, though acting, he is not bound. (23) The one whose attachments are gone, who is liberated, whose mind is established in knowledge, who works for the sake of sacrifice, eradicates the binding effect of action.

(24) He, who believes that the act of offering is *Brahman*, the offering itself is *Brahman*, the one who pours the offering into the fire of *Brahman* is *Brahman*; and in this way all activity is *Brahman*, attains *Brahman*. (25) Some perform sacrifices to the deities; while others offer the self as sacrifice by the Self in the fire of *Brahman*. (26) Others restrain the cognitive senses as an offering into the fire; and others offer the objects of the senses into the fire of the sense organs. (27) And others offer the actions of the senses and vital breath of the Yoga of self-restraint, which is lit by the fire of knowledge. (28) Similarly, others offer wealth,

austerities, and Yoga practices; while some others practice self-restraint and stern vows and study the scriptures and other knowledge as an offering. (29) Others practicing *prānayāma*, regulate the breath and vital energy, offering their *apāna* (outgoing breath) into their *prāna* (incoming breath) or the *prāna* into the *apāna*. (30) Others restrict their food and offer the life breath into the life breath; all these are knowers of sacrifice and have their sins consumed by sacrifice. (31) Those enjoyers of the nectar remaining after sacrifice attain the eternal *Brahman*. This world is not for the non-performers of sacrifice, how then the other, Arjuna. (32) In this way, many kinds of offerings are spread out before *Brahman*. Know them all to be born of action. When you have acquired this knowledge then you will obtain release. (33) The wisdom sacrifice is superior to the sacrifice of material possessions Arjuna. All actions of all kinds culminate in knowledge.

(34) Know this: Through humble submission, through enquiry, and through service, those who have realized truth will instruct you in that knowledge. (35) Knowing that, Arjuna, you shall not again be overcome by mental confusion like this, and by that knowledge you will see all beings in your Self and also in Me. (36) Even if you are the most sinful among all the sinful, you will sail over all sin by the ship of knowledge. (37) Just as kindled fire reduces fuel to ashes, Arjuna, the fire of knowledge reduces all actions to ashes.

(38) For, in this world, there is nothing as pure as knowledge. In time, that pure knowledge is attained, within oneself, by the person who has mastered Yoga. (39) The person having faith, who is intent upon it, and who has mastered his senses, attains knowledge. Having attained knowledge, one quickly attains supreme peace. (40) The person, without knowledge, faith, and who is constantly full of doubt, is destroyed. For the doubter, there is neither this world, nor the next, nor any happiness.

(41) Actions do not bind the one who lives this Yoga, whose doubts are rent asunder by knowledge, and who is self-possessed, Arjuna. (42) Therefore, with the sword of knowledge, cut asunder this doubt regarding the Self that is present in your heart resulting from ignorance. Take shelter in this Yoga and rise up.

Chapter V
Renunciation

Krishna has clearly stated there are two paths. Arjuna wants to know which of the two is superior, and therefore the one he should follow. Krishna tells him that the path of action, called Yoga, is superior to the renunciation of action as it will lead more quickly to the highest good. He then clarifies what it means to be established in renunciation—above liking and disliking. Liking and disliking are qualities inherent with the ego, the individual doer, and are active because of our identification of our soul with this limited form.

He explains that when renunciation is firmly established, both the path of Sāmkhya and the path of Yoga lead to the same result: absolute freedom, bliss and tranquility. Krishna then details what renunciation means for the person on the path of action and then describes at the end of the chapter how the ascetic attains the same goal.

Slokas

Arjuna said: (1) O Krishna, you praise renunciation of actions and again you praise Yoga, the performance of actions. Tell me definitely which is superior of the two.

Śri Krishna said: (2) Both, renunciation and the Yoga of action lead to the highest good. Of these two, the Yoga of action is superior to the renunciation of action. (3) He is established in renunciation who neither desires nor hates [likes and dislikes]; for he who has been liberated from the pairs of opposites is easily liberated from the bonds of action. (4) The childish, not the wise, declare Sāmkhya and Yoga as distinct. He who is established in the practice of one, gains the fruit of both. (5) The state that is attained by the followers of Sāmkhya is also attained by the followers of Yoga. One, who sees Sāmkhya and Yoga as one, sees the truth. (6) O might-armed Arjuna, renunciation is difficult to achieve without Yoga.

The disciplined practitioner, following the path of disinterested action, quickly attains the Supreme Self.

(7) One, who is steeped in this Yoga of action, whose motive is pure, who has mastered their mind and senses, and realized the one Self that dwells within all beings, is not tainted even when acting. (8-9) Steadfast in Yoga, the knower of truth should realize, "I do nothing at all." Whether seeing, hearing, touching, smelling, eating, walking, sleeping, breathing, speaking, excreting, grasping, and opening and closing the eyes, he understands the senses are interacting with their respective objects.

(10) One who performs actions without attachment, dedicating them to *Brahman* (Supreme Self) is not tainted by sin, just as water does not adhere to a lotus leaf. (11) A follower of Yoga performs action only with the body, mind, senses and intellect, forsaking attachment, for self-purification. (12) The stable-minded one, who is steeped in Yoga, having giving up the fruits of action, attains complete tranquility. The undisciplined one, driven by desire and attached to the fruits of actions, is firmly bound. (13) The embodied one, having renounced all actions by discrimination, rests happily in the city of nine gates, doing nothing and causing nothing to be done.

(14) The Lord does not create the authorship, the actions of individuals, or the connection between the actions and their fruits; it is the inherent tendencies of nature (*prakriti*) that does it all. (15) The all-pervading One does not receive the merit or demerit of anyone. As knowledge is enveloped by nescience, thus all beings are deluded. (16) But for those whose blindness is destroyed by the knowledge of the Self; that knowledge, like the sun, illuminates the Supreme. (17) Those whose intellect has become engrossed in that Supreme, whose minds find happiness in it, who become established in that, and hold that as their highest goal, have their impurities cleansed by knowledge and are released from the cycle of birth and death.

(18) The knowers of the Self look with an equal eye on the learned endowed with humility, a cow, an elephant, and even a dog or an outcaste. (19) Those whose mind has become steady in this evenness conquer mortal existence even in this life, since the *Brahman* (Supreme Self) is the same in all and is without blemish. Therefore, they rest in the *Brahman*.

(20) Resting in *Brahman*, with the intellect steady and without misconception, the knower of *Brahman* neither rejoices on attaining what

is pleasant, nor is shaken by what is unpleasant. (21) One who is unattached to external sensations obtains the happiness which resides in *Brahman*. Such a person, whose Self is one with *Brahman*, attains unending happiness. (22) But pleasure, born of contacts with external objects, has a beginning and ending; and becomes the cause of unhappiness. (23) One, who can withstand in this life the agitation arising from desire and anger even here before leaving the body, is liberated and is a happy person. (24) One whose happiness is from within, who has found tranquility within, and who is illuminated from within, that *yogin* becoming *Brahman*-formed rises above limitation and attains the bliss of *Brahman*. (25) The seers, who have lost the sense of duality, whose doubts are dispelled, whose senses are under control, engaged in the welfare of all beings, attain absolute freedom.

(26) For the ascetic who is free from desire and anger, who has controlled his thought, and who knows the Self, the bliss of *Brahman* exists everywhere. (27-28) Shutting out contact with external objects, fixing the gaze between the eyebrows, equalizing the inhalation and exhalation passing through the nostrils, controlling the senses, mind and intellect, having liberation as the supreme goal, free from desire, fear and anger, is forever liberated. (29) Having known Me—the Lord of all sacrifices and austerities, the Lord of all worlds, the friend of all beings—he attains peace.

Chapter VI
Meditation

Pure knowledge, which leads to peace, is attained by realization of the Self. Krishna explains that this same goal is reached whether one follows the path of Sāmkhya or that of Yoga, but that He considers Yoga, the path of action, to be superior. Krishna's emphasis has been on the development of a stable intellect: a one-pointed focus gained by relinquishing or renouncing the fruits of action, but not action itself. In the third chapter, He cites the examples of King Janaka and others as those who attained release by performing action for universal welfare. In the fourth chapter, He explains how He Himself takes birth in different ages for the purpose of protecting the good, destroying the wicked, and for establishing right action once again. Though He is unborn, imperishable, and the Lord of all beings, by governing His own nature (*prakriti*) He is born by His own divine power.

Krishna speaks to Arjuna and to us from His position as the manifested form of *Brahman* called *Īśvara* or Godhead. *Brahman*, the Supreme Self, is beyond description, yet manifests or becomes known through His own divine power. Patanjali describes *Īśvara* as a special kind of *purusha* (Self) untouched by misery, action, and the results of action.[11] He is omniscient, incomparable, unlimited, all-pervasive and the abode of knowledge. According to Vedanta philosophy we are in the image or likeness of Godhead, but we have been touched by misery, action, the results of action, and have an unknown accumulation of *karma* in store for the future.

Krishna continues by explaining that the person who knows the truth underlying His divine births and actions is not born again after leaving the body. In other words with full knowledge one gains release. Our Self is free from birth and it is the attributes of *prakriti* that are responsible for

---

[11] *Yoga Sūtras* I-24.

action. The Self remains untouched and in its own position as the attributes of *prakriti* act amongst themselves. With this understanding and full knowledge, peace is attained.

Krishna describes how desire, which is housed in the senses, mind, and intellect, is the enemy and enshrouds our knowledge and discrimination. These impressions of desire, which are structured in the intellect, are the driving force behind our actions. They overwhelm our discrimination and throw us into confusion. Krishna advises us to gain control of our senses and destroy this enemy of our Self. He tells us that we ourselves are responsible for our upliftment and degradation, and that we must learn to be our own helper, and not our own enemy.

The sixth chapter concerns the development of self-discipline. Within the chapter, *ātma* and its derivations are used when indicating different components of self. *Ātma* and its derivations can mean soul, self, intellect, mind, ego, the body or the full person. For example, *ātmana* means intellect and *ātmanam* means mind. *Parātman* can mean the Supreme Self or the highest self in the body. Many translations use "self" for all these references instead of identifying the intended specific component of self. Swami Bawra emphasized the necessary understanding of the specific word usage and placement to gain the meaning of the specific *sloka*.

In the seventh chapter Krishna states,

> Earth, water, fire, air, ether, the mind (*manas*), intellect (*buddhi*) and individuation (*ahamkāra*)—thus my material nature is divided eightfold. This is my inferior nature. But know this as distinct from my higher nature, the life element (*jīvabhūtām*) by which this universe is maintained. Know that all beings have these two as the source of their birth.

We all have a higher and lower nature, and it is important to understand how these elements work in our lives and constitute our selves.

The five elements introduced constitute the physical form of every being and of the physical world. At this point in the conversation Krishna indicates only mind, but later he will describe the mind as one of eleven senses, which include the five active and five cognitive senses.[12] Therefore, in this sloka mind includes the sensual input as well. In

---

[12] *Bhagavad Gītā* XIII/5.

addition, we have ego, intellect, and a higher nature, which is our life element (*jīvabhūtām*). The Upanishads discuss *chitta*, *buddhi*, *ahamkara*, and *manas*. Together these projections of nature are called the *antah-karana*, our inner faculty of knowing. The practice of meditation is advised as the means for understanding our higher nature and the faculties of intellect, ego and mind.

Chitta is the seed of our life. It is the medium for receiving, holding and manifesting the qualities of the Supreme Self. When the qualities of the Supreme Self are adopted by the medium of *chitta* our higher nature is formed. This is the life element, *jīvabhūtām* or the individual soul, *jīvātma*. It is the embodied self and the highest self in the body. We have an individual experience because of the individual quality of the medium intermingling with the Supreme Self.

In addition to holding the qualities of the Supreme, the medium holds our experienced knowledge. The *chitta* is similar to a tiny silicon computer chip that is capable of holding a vast number of instructions. Our individual *chitta* is infinitesimally smaller than a computer chip, yet holds millions of impressions from our previous lives. These impressions structure our intelligence and are the cause of our belief system, abilities, actions, and current physical form.

When this medium is enlivened it activates the impressions that then form our intellect. Our thinking and deciding capabilities are determined by these impressions. This may be compared to an electrical appliance that is activated by electricity. The appliance operates according to its programming and components. Our intellect controls the mind, the senses, and the body, propelling them into activity. This discriminative and determinative faculty sanctions all activities. The intellect prompts the mind and the senses to work through the gross vehicle of the body. All actions are preceded by motives that appear in the waves of the mind. Therefore, Krishna will tell us that the intellect is responsible for our upliftment or degradation.

Ego is the active power of our inner faculty. Krishna calls it the doer. Its purpose is to act on behalf of the Supreme Self. It is only because of the misunderstanding of this component, and the acceptance of our existence as one of a limited entity, that a process of liking and disliking, desire and anger is initiated. We begin to accept and reject the objects and persons we encounter. The egoistic self is expressed as thoughts, feelings and emotions.

The mind is both volitional and perceptual. *Manas* is an instrument of cognition. The volitional quality of the mind is the egoistic self. The perceptual aspect of the mind is the mind's connection with the cognitive senses. Each sense collects information: ears collect sound; skin collects touch; eyes collect form; tongue collects taste; and nose smells. This information is collated and displayed in the mind as thoughts and images.

In essence the intellect, ego, and mind are inseparable and indivisible. They are the different modifications of the medium, *chitta*. Our entire existence depends upon the Supreme Self. When the *chitta* is enlivened with the qualities of the Supreme Self, it becomes active and modifies into these three functions. First, the *chitta* produces our discriminative faculty, the intellect. Then, our I-amness, called the *aham*, manifests from the experience of the individual medium that is holding our sense of existence. Krishna calls this *jivabhūtam*. Depending on our spiritual development, I-amness either accepts itself as the manifestation of the Supreme Self within this medium, or it accepts the limited form of the medium as itself. Impurity leads to this mistaken identity. When I-amness accepts the limited, individual form of the medium, it functions within this boundary of individual existence called *ahamkara* or ego. As our awareness extends outside of this medium, we experience waves of thought called *manas* or mind.

Practice and detachment serve to quiet and purify our *antah-karana*. Patanjali states, "Yoga is the stilling of the modifications of chitta."[13] When we reach this still state, "Then the seer abides in itself."[14] In other words, our individual existence is realized as one with the Supreme Self. Krishna says, "Those whose intellects pursue the Self, whose minds dwell upon it, who undergo discipline for it, and hold it as the highest object, have their impurities cleansed by knowledge and achieve the highest goal."[15] Our efforts prepare the instruments of the *antah-karana* to receive the grace of the Supreme Self and realize its glory. Meditation is the means by which we develop toward this realization.

---

[13] *Yoga Sūtras* I/2.
[14] *Yoga Sūtras* I/3.
[15] *Bhagavad Gītā* V/17.

Krishna begins by defining renunciation as Yoga because no one can attain the Self without renouncing selfish purpose, that is, by performing good works without expectation of their fruit. Renunciation or self-restraint is accomplished through discipline, gained through the proper understanding of our insturments of perception and action. He advises us to take responsibility for our development and describes the practice of meditation and the optimum lifestyle for sustaining our practice.

Slokas

Śri Krishna said: (1) The person, who performs works that ought to be done without expecting their fruit, is a *sannyāsin* (renunciant) and *yogin*; not the one who is without a sacred fire and performs no action. (2) O Arjuna, understand that what is known as renunciation is Yoga, because no one becomes a *yogi* without renouncing selfish purpose.

(3) For the learned desirous of attaining yoga, action is said to be the means; for the one who has already attained yoga, serenity is said to be the means. (4) Because when a person is not attached to sense-objects or to action, and relinquishes all thoughts, then one is said to have attained yoga.

(5) One should take responsibility for one's own upliftment; one should not diminish or degrade oneself; for you alone are your own helper or your own enemy. (6) One who has mastered the mind with the intellect becomes his own helper, but for whom the mind is not conquered; it acts against him like an enemy.

(7) The indwelling Self of him, who has subdued the mind and attained tranquility, is steadfast in cold, heat, pleasure, and pain, as well as honor and dishonor. (8) The *yogi*, whose intellect has become satisfied with knowledge [of the Supreme Self] and wisdom [discriminative knowledge gained from personal experience], whose mind is stable and senses are under control, and looks upon the earth, stone and gold as the same, is said to be united with the Supreme Self. (9) He who looks with an equal eye upon well-wishers, friends, foes, the indifferent, neutrals, the hateful, relatives, and upon the righteous and unrighteous is distinguished among humans.

(10) The practitioner of Yoga should concentrate constantly on the Self, remaining alone in a solitary place, with the mind and the body controlled, free from desires and the sense of possession. (11-12) Having

established a firm seat in a pure place, not too high or too low, and covered with a cloth, a skin and kusha grass, there, sitting on the seat, with the mind focused internally and allowing the thoughts and activity of the senses to quiet, practice Yoga for the purification of the self. (13) Holding the trunk, head and neck erect motionless and steady, without looking around, fix the gaze on the tip of the nose. (14) With a quieted mind, not entertaining any fear, turning one's emotions inwardly and fixing one's thoughts on Me, sit intent on Me as the Supreme. (15) Thus, continuing this practice, the mind becomes subdued, and the practitioner, attains the supreme peace of oneness, which abides in Me.

(16) O Arjuna, one who eats too much or eats nothing, and who sleeps too much or keeps awake too long cannot succeed in this Yoga. (17) For the person who is moderate in food and recreation, whose action is not excessive, and for whose sleeping and wakefulness is measured, Yoga becomes a destroyer of all sorrows. (18) When the disciplined mind rests in the Self alone, free from longing for any object of desire, then a practitioner is said to be established in Yoga. (19) Just as a lamp placed in a windless spot does not flicker, similarly the disciplined mind is stable for the practitioner of Yoga.

(20) When the *chitta* comes to rest, with the mind restrained by the practice of Yoga, and one beholds the Supreme Self as the self, one becomes content in the Self alone. (21) When one knows that infinite happiness which can be grasped by the intellect, but is beyond the senses, and the intellect becomes steady in that, one does not sway from that reality. (22) Having attained this, no greater gain can be imagined; established in this, one is not moved even by heavy sorrow. (23) Let this severance from union with pain be known as Yoga. This Yoga is to be practiced with determination and with a mind free from despondency.

(24-25) Abandoning all desires born of volition and restraining the senses on all sides by the mind; gradually, one should withdraw oneself from the objects with the help of a firmly resolved intellect; and steadying the mind on the Self one should think of nothing else. (26) Whenever the restless and unsteady mind wanders, one should restrain it and bring it within the control of the intellect. (27) The practitioner, whose mind is peaceful, whose passions are calmed, who is free of evil and has become one with the Supreme Self, attains the highest bliss. (28) The *yogi*, who continually practices in this fashion, becomes freed from all impurities and easily attains the infinite bliss of contact with the Supreme Self.

(29) He whose mind is made steadfast by Yoga sees equality everywhere; he sees the same Supreme Self abiding in all beings and all beings present in one Supreme Self. (30) He who sees Me everywhere and sees everything in Me, such a one never becomes separated from Me, nor do I become separated from him. (31) The *yogi* who, being established in unity, worships me dwelling in all beings, no matter in what mode of life he chooses abides in Me. (32) O Arjuna, that *yogi* who sees everywhere that others are the same as himself, whether in pleasure or pain, is regarded as superior.

Arjuna said: (33) O Krishna, this Yoga declared by you as equability of reason, I do not see its lasting endurance because of the restlessness of the mind. (34) For the mind is volatile, turbulent, strong and obstinate. I think it is as difficult to control as the wind.

Śri Krishna said: (35) O Arjuna, without a doubt the mind is restless and difficult to restrain; but through practice and dispassion it can be brought under control. (36) I agree that yoga is difficult to attain for that person whose inner sense (*antah-karana*) is uncontrolled. However, it can be attained through proper means when one makes the effort to skillfully use their intellect, ego and mind.

Arjuna said: (37) O Krishna, what happens to the person who is unable to control himself but has faith, whose mind moves away from yoga and then fails to attain success in Yoga? (38) Does such a person, fallen from both [worldly happiness and spiritual perfection], confused in the path of attaining the Supreme Self, perish without support like a broken cloud? (39) O Krishna, you must completely dispel this doubt of mine; for it is not possible for any but you to remove this doubt.

Śri Krishna said: (40) Arjuna, such a person does not come to grief either in this world, or in the next world; because no person who performs beneficial actions ever reaches an unhappy end, my son. (41) Having attained the worlds of the doers of meritorious deeds, and dwelling there for long years, one fallen from yoga is born in the home of the pure and prosperous. (42) Or one may be born in the family of wise *yogis*, but such a birth is difficult to obtain in this world. (43) There, one is united with the knowledge acquired in his former body and strives onward once more toward perfection. (44) By the momentum of his previous practice, he is carried forward even against his will. He who even wishes to know of Yoga goes beyond the performance of Vedic rituals. (45) Through persevering effort, the one who has resorted to Yoga becomes cleansed of impurities, perfected through many births, and then attains the highest state.

(46) The *yogi* is superior to those who practice austerities, to those who possess knowledge, and to those who are devoted to ritual activities. O Arjuna, become a *yogi*. (47) Of all *yogis*, the one full of faith, who worships Me with his inner self abiding in Me, I consider him the greatest among *yogis*.

Chapter VII
Knowledge and Realization

Arjuna has expressed a doubt as to whether the Yoga of equanimity could be maintained given the restless nature of the mind. His concern was that if effort were applied and success was not attained, then the aspirant would gain neither material happiness nor the benefit of a spiritual quest. For this reason, he has asked Krishna to completely dispel his doubt and to assure him of the value of this pursuit.

Krishna responds by clarifying in Chapter VI, that every person receives the merit generated by their virtuous actions in their current lifetime, as well as that of attaining heavenly existence. But according to Vedic teaching, although the result of virtuous work is heavenly enjoyment, heaven is temporary. In heaven, we enjoy the results of our previous actions, but we cannot perform additional worthy actions. Therefore, when the results of virtue have been exhausted, we take birth again. Krishna assures Arjuna that a practitioner on the path of Yoga will gain a favorable birth, whereby the knowledge and experience of his practice will continue from the point of his departure.

Now begins a discussion on how all manifestation springs from one source, revealing the unity underlying this diverse creation. The One manifests into a higher and lower nature: a higher, conscious life principle that sustains all forms, yet remains distinct from them; and lower material expressions. All beings have this same constitution—we are a projection of the eternal One. We have the same properties as our Source. Everything originates from the One and exists within the One, yet the One, though all-pervading is beyond all limitation. The One is infinite.

Some have described this manifested world as an illusion. They call it *māyā*, and teach that the world is not real and does not exist. But *māyā* is the divine power of the Supreme Lord that enables the indescribable to become describable. In Sanskrit *mā* means "measure" and *yā* means "who." *Māyā* is the divine power providing the means to measure immeasurable infinity. In other words, *māyā* limits the immeasurable into forms that can be seen and understood. *Māyā* is the infinite power of the Supreme Self. It is inseparable and indistinguishable from *Brahman*. "Know then that *prakriti* is *māyā* and the master of *māyā* is the Supreme Lord. The whole world is pervaded by beings that are part of Him."[16] The world exists as a manifestation of *Brahman*. *Māyā* manifests this omnipresent, immeasurable Supreme Self into our individual form. Illusion is the mistaken belief that we are separate from *Brahman*.

Many commentators believe Krishna begins a discussion on Bhakti Yoga, devotion, starting with Chapter VII. They consider the teaching of the *Bhagavad Gītā* to be divided into three parts. The first six chapters are a discussion on *Karma* Yoga—the path of action, the next six chapters deal with *Bhakti* Yoga—the path of devotion, and the last six chapters emphasize *Jñāna* Yoga—the path of knowledge. Tilak disagrees with this division. He states that although all of these topics are discussed, they are not independent of the one system of Yoga taught by Krishna to Arjuna.

In Chapter III, Krishna states that desire and anger become fixed in the intellect, ego, mind and senses and destroy our knowledge and discrimination. He indicates the necessity of gaining control of the senses in order to overcome desire and anger and to live the path of desireless action, Yoga. In Chapter VI, He offers the practice of meditation as the means to accomplish self-control and told Arjuna that the accomplished practitioner, a true *yogi*, who has gained control of his senses, sees the Supreme Self in all beings and all beings in the Supreme Self. In Chapter VI, we see that such a person is satisfied with his knowledge, *jñāna*, and wisdom, *vijñāna*.

Realizing that there is only one imperishable Supreme Self which pervades all manifested worlds is known as *jñāna*, and understanding how diversity comes into existence as an expression of the Supreme Source is known as *vijñāna*. The Supreme Self has two aspects: the imperceptible and the perceptible, the immutable and the mutable. The imperceptible, unchanging aspect is realizable by reason, and the perceptible, mutable aspect is known through direct experience and observation.

The eleven chapters that follow elucidate these two aspects of the Supreme in order to help purify and develop our reasoning and discrimination. *Jñāna*, the realization of one Supreme Self pervading all,

---

[16] *Śvetāśvatara Upanishad* IV.10.

dwelling within us as our individual existence; and *vijñāna*, fully understanding that all we see, including our own self and every other being, originates in and manifests from the same Supreme Source. Devotion is accepting our role and purpose in this unfoldment and learning to participate fully within a divine manifestation.

Both knowledge and devotion are indeed supportive and essential on the path of Yoga. We need both to realize the Supreme Self and to refine our discrimination in order to make the choices that will allow divinity to manifest through our lives. These are not independent parts of this teaching, but are integrated into the single path of desireless action called Yoga.

Slokas

Śrī Krishna said: (1) O Arjuna, hear how you will acquire complete and doubtless knowledge of Me while you are absorbed in Me, practicing Yoga and taking shelter in Me. (2) I will fully explain this knowledge along with realization, after knowing which nothing more here remains to be known. (3) Only a handful of persons out of thousands make an attempt to attain perfection; and out of those making an attempt, only a few gain true knowledge of Me.

(4) Earth, water, fire, air, ether, the mind (*manah*), intellect (*buddhi*) and individuation (*ahamkārah*)—thus my material nature is divided eightfold. (5) This is my inferior nature, Arjuna. But know this as distinct from my higher nature, the life element (*jīvabhūtām*) by which this universe is maintained. (6) Know that all beings have these two as the source of their birth. Therefore, I am the origin and the end of this entire universe. (7) There is nothing higher than Myself, Arjuna. All this is strung on Me, like gems on a thread.

(8) I am the liquidity in water, Arjuna; I am the radiance in the sun and moon, the sacred syllable (Om) in all the Vedas, the sound in ether and virility in man. (9) I am the sweet fragrance in the earth and the brilliance in fire, the life in all beings, and I am the austerity of ascetics. (10) Know me, Arjuna, as the eternal seed of all beings. I am the intelligence of the discerning, and the brilliance of the brilliant. (11) In the strong, I am strength, devoid of desire and passion, and in all beings I am the sensual longing, which is in accord with righteousness. (12) Whatever beings and

objects that are pure, active and inert (*sāttvic, rājasic,* and *tāmasic*) proceed from Me. They are in Me, yet I am not in them.

(13) This entire universe, deluded by these three states of being composed of the constituents of nature (*prakriti*), does not realize Me, who is beyond them and immutable. (14) My divine *māyā*, composed of the three *gunas*, is difficult to overcome; only those who take refuge in Me can cross beyond this *māyā*. (15) The fools and evil-doers, the lowest of men, do not seek Me; they whose knowledge is destroyed by *māyā* follow the ways of demons.

(16) Four kinds of virtuous men worship Me: the distressed, those who desire knowledge, those who desire wealth, and the person of wisdom [the realized one], O Arjuna. (17) Of them the person of wisdom, eternally steadfast, and devoted to Me alone, is prominent. I am most beloved of the person of wisdom and he is beloved of Me. (18) All these are good, but I hold the realized one to be My very Self; for he is united with Me and has become steady in Me, the highest goal. (19) After many births, the person of wisdom reaches Me, realizing that all this is Vāsudeva (Supreme Self). Such a noble soul is rare.

(20) Others controlled by their inherent nature and deprived of discrimination due to various desires, observe various rites and worship other deities. (21) Whatever form or deity any devotee seeks to worship with faith, I make that very faith steadfast. (22) Endowed with that faith, he worships that form and thence gets the objects of his desire provided in reality by Me alone. (23) But the fruit gained by these people of limited understanding is perishable; those who worship deities, reach the deities, and those who worship Me, come to Me.

(24) Not knowing my supreme state, imperishable and unsurpassed, the foolish look upon Me, though imperceptible, as having become perceptible. (25) As I am veiled by My divine *māyā*, I do not appear to all. This deluded world does not recognize Me, the unborn and imperishable. (26) I know all beings, Arjuna, past, present and those to come; but no one knows Me. (27) All beings fall into delusion at birth, Arjuna, because of the confusion created by the pairs of opposites springing from desire and aversion. (28) But virtuous individuals, whose sin is exhausted, escaping from the delusion created by the pairs of opposites, become fixed in purpose and worship Me.

(29) Those who take refuge in Me and strive for deliverance from old age and death, realize in full that *Brahman* (Supreme Self), the individual self, and all action. (30) Those, who realize Me in the *adhibhūta* (physical region), in the *adhidaiva* (divine region) and in the *adhiyajña* (region of sacrifice), they of steadfast wisdom realize Me even at the hour of death.

Chapter VIII
Imperishable *Brahman*

In accord with the Upanishads, Vedanta holds the position that there is only one, imperishable, Supreme Self, *Paramātman* or *Brahman*, which pervades all created beings (*adhibhūta*), all sacrifices (*adhiyajña*), all deities (*adhidaiva*), and whose intrinsic quality is to dwell within all individual bodies as self (*adhyātma*). *Brahman* is the origin of all action (karma) through its divine power, *māyā*, which causes the emergence and growth of all beings.

Here, Krishna explains these different aspects of Imperishable *Brahman* in response to Arjuna's questions. He describes the value and importance of holding a vision of the Supreme Self in our minds at all times, especially at the moment of death.

Slokas

Arjuna said: (1) O best among men, what is that *Brahman*? What is *adhyātma*? What is *karma*? What is called *adhibhūta*, and what is called *adhidaiva*? (2) Who and what is *adhiyajña* in this body, Krishna? And how do those, who control the senses, realize you at the moment of death?

Śri Krishna said: (3) That, which is supreme and imperishable, is *Brahman*. Its intrinsic quality [dwelling in every individual body] is called *adhyātma*. The creative power which causes the origin and growth of beings is called *karma*. (4) The perishable aspect of existence is called *adhibhūta*, and the *purusha* [indwelling self or soul] is the *adhidaiva*. I alone am the *adhiyajña* [lord of sacrifice] here in this body.

(5) And there is no doubt that he who leaves his body, remembering Me at the moment of death, attains to My being. (6) O Arjuna, whatever form a person thinks of at the last moment when he leaves his body, having been engrossed in thinking of that form, that alone does he attain. (7) Therefore, think of Me at all times and fight. With mind and intellect fixed on Me, you will surely come to Me. (8) O Arjuna, when a person,

with the help of constant practice, steadies his mind, not letting it wander after anything else, and meditates on the resplendent, Supreme *Purusha* (Self), he reaches Him.

(9-10) The practitioner who meditates on the *Purusha*—the omniscient, the ancient, the ruler, smaller than an atom, the sustainer of all, of inconceivable form, who is effulgent like the sun, and beyond the darkness of ignorance—at the time of death, with a steady mind, endowed with devotion and the power of Yoga, fixing the *prāna* (life-breath) in the middle of the two eyebrows, he reaches that effulgent, Supreme Self.

(11) I will briefly describe to you that goal, which the knowers of the Veda call the Imperishable, which the ascetics—free from passion—enter, and desiring which they practice the vow of celibacy. (12-13) Controlling all the gates of the body [the senses], and confining the mind in the heart, having fixed the life-breath in the head [*hrdi*, heart, indicates the *brahma chakra* at the top of the head], engaged in the practice of Yoga concentration, meditating on *Om*—the one-syllable form of *Brahman*—and thinking upon me, he who departs, leaving the body, attains the supreme goal.

(14) Arjuna, I am easily attainable by that ever steadfast *yogi*, who remembers Me constantly with a feeling that there is none other than Me. (15) Reaching the highest perfection and having attained Me, these great souls are not subject to rebirth, which is the place of unhappiness and is non-permanent. (16) All worlds, including that of *Brahmā*, are subject to return, Arjuna, but on reaching me, O son of Kunti, there is no rebirth.

(17) Those who know that the day of *Brahmā* lasts a thousand *yugas* and that his night lasts a thousand *yugas*, they are the knowers of day and night. (18) At the coming of the day all manifest beings proceed from the unmanifest, and at the coming of night they dissolve into that alone which is called the unmanifested, *avyakta*. (19) Arjuna, this multitude of beings, coming forth again and again, is dissolved, in spite of themselves, when the night starts, and they come forth again when the day starts.

(20) But beyond this unmanifested, there is yet another unmanifest Eternal Existence, which does not perish when all beings perish. (21) That unmanifest is called the Imperishable, *Aksara*. It is said to be the ultimate state. Those who attain It, return not. That is My supreme abode. (22) O Arjuna, that highest *Purusha* (Self), within whom all beings dwell and by whom all this is pervaded, can be reached only by devotion to Him alone.

(23) Now, I will mention to you, Arjuna, the time in which the *yogis* depart never to return and also the time in which they depart to return. (24) Fire, light, daytime, the bright half of the moon, and the six months of the northern path of the sun—departing then, those knowers of *Brahman* (Supreme Self) go to *Brahman*. (25) Smoke, night, the dark half of the moon, and the six months of the southern passage of the sun—departing then, the *yogi* obtains the lunar light and returns. (26) The bright and the dark paths of the world are thought to be eternal. By one path a person departs and does not return, and by the other he returns.

(27) Arjuna, no *yogi* who understands these two paths is deluded. Therefore, Arjuna, be steadfast in Yoga at all times. (28) The *yogi* who understands this transcends the fruits of meritorious deeds attached to the study of the Vedas, sacrifices, austerities and gifts, and reaches the highest state which lies beyond.

Chapter IX
The Sovereign Science and the Sovereign Secret

Now, the highest knowledge—the deepest philosophical and mystical secret—will be explained by Krishna. This knowledge combined with the direct experience of realization frees us from the bondage of ignorance (sin). The experience of realization transforms secondhand knowledge into firsthand knowledge. In this way, scriptural knowledge, often heard from a teacher, becomes internal wisdom. This knowing, untouched by doubt, forms a firm resolve, or faith, within us.

The Vedas say that *Brahman*, the Supreme Self, is beyond description. It is indicated as *satyam jñānam anantam*.[17] *Satyam* means eternal truth; *jñānam* means pure knowledge; and *anantam* is infinity. We experience *satyam* as existence, *jñānam* as intelligence, and *anantam* as bliss. Bliss is the experience of not being bound, limited or finite. In this state, our sense of self experiences an expansiveness—the bliss of *Brahman*. In Chapter VIII, Krishna taught, "That highest *Purusha* (Supreme Self), within whom all beings dwell and by whom all this is pervaded, can be reached only by devotion to Him alone."

In this chapter, Krishna explains the mystery of all-pervasiveness and our experience of it as His divine Yoga, by saying, "This universe is pervaded by My unmanifest aspect. All beings exist in Me [Supreme Self], but I am not in them. And yet, beings do not abide in Me. Behold My divine Yoga. Bringing forth and supporting all beings, My Self, does not dwell in them." Then He provides an example whereby we might understand this mystery, "As the mighty wind, which moves everywhere, rests eternally in space, similarly understand that all beings rest in Me."

"Activating My own *prakriti*, material nature, I project again and again this multitude of beings." *Chitta* is the first projection of *prakriti*. It is the seed of every individual being. In Chapter XV, Krishna says, "Merely a

---

17 *Taittirīya Upanishad* II.1.2

fragment of Myself becomes the eternal *jīvabhūta*, individual life element." *Chitta* is a medium for receiving, holding and manifesting the all-pervasive qualities of the Supreme Self. When the qualities of the Supreme Self are adopted by the medium of *chitta*, our higher nature is formed. We have an individual experience of existence because of the individual quality of the medium.

But, *purusha* does not become divided or limited, as it pervades and dwells within and without every medium. The Self is always one, indivisible, imperishable and immutable, even as it passes through a medium. The *Katha Upanishad* explains, "Just as air resides in various forms in the universe, in the same way one Supreme *Brahman* manifests Himself in the form of many individual souls and is the same in and out."[18] Krishna says, "Behold My divine Yoga." He gives the example of wind, which while moving everywhere, always rests in space. Likewise, our mediums are in constant motion, but always reside in the all-pervasive Supreme Self, which remains the same in and out.

The presence of Self is similar to the way in which space is all-pervading, existing both inside and outside of all containers. It seems as if space is defined by specific containers, but the containers merely define the boundaries of one space. Space dwells within and without a building. Buildings appear to divide space, but space is indivisible. We may believe that all-pervading existence, experienced as our individual existence, is specific to us, but it is in fact part and parcel of the all-pervading Self. Just as we define space by the boundaries we create, we define our existence by the boundary of the *chitta*, and so we superimpose limits on the Self.

The Supreme Self cannot be limited by this medium. Rather, it enlightens the medium and pervades all existence. The medium has limits, but the Self does not. The Supreme Self enlightens all *chittas* and yet it exists above and beyond all bodies because it remains distinctly unmixed in the material world, while it is, at the same time, the substratum of the whole universe. Again the *Katha Upanishad* provides a simile, "Just as the sun gives light to the eyes and is not affected by the defects of the eyes, in the same way one Supreme *Brahman*, even being the soul of all bodies, is never polluted by their pains [mortality, limitation, finiteness, and a sense of lack]."

---

[18] *Katha Upanishad* 2.3.10.

Space is indivisible, but there are countless objects, such as pots and houses, that have space within them and appear to limit space. The various containers create the appearance of confining space, but space is everywhere, within and beyond all limitations. In the same way, *purusha* is one, even as it appears as many in the countless forms enlightened by the Supreme Self. Later, in Chapter XIII, Krishna says, "truly that Supreme Self is indivisible but when manifested in numerous forms, looks as if divided."[19]

To live with an unshakeable faith in our existence as wholly dependent upon, and completely integrated with the Supreme Self, is the most rewarding challenge of human life. It is the deepening of this experience, called devotion, which draws the qualities of the Supreme Self into our lives, and into a vision whereby we reach the Supreme Self. With the practice of devotion we make the imperceptible perceptible by means of love.

According to Tilak, this path of devotion is not separate, but an integral aspect of the knowledge and wisdom needed for living the path of desireless action described by Krishna as Yoga. He will emphasize that we must fix our minds upon, honor and be devoted to the Supreme Self, and thus remain steadfast with the Supreme Self as our aim. In this way we will more easily reach the highest goal.

Slokas

Śrī Krishna said: (1) Now, as you do not cavil [make petty objections], I shall declare to you the most secret knowledge combined with direct experience [realization], knowing which, you will be free from all sin. (2) This is the sovereign science, the royal mystery, the supreme purifier. It is instinctively experienced, consistent with ethical and moral principles, easy to practice and imperishable. (3) Those persons, Arjuna, who do not have faith in this *dharma* (behaviors that uphold life) do not attain Me, but return to the path of worldly life, fraught with mortality.

(4) This whole universe is pervaded by My unmanifest aspect. All beings exist in Me [*Paramātman* or Supreme Self], but I am not in them. (5) And yet, beings do not abide in Me. Behold by My divine Yoga. Bringing forth and supporting all beings, My Self, does not dwell in them. (6) As

---

[19] *Bhagavad Gītā* XIII-16.

the mighty wind, which moves everywhere, rests eternally in space, similarly understand that all beings rest in Me.

(7) Arjuna, at the end of a *kalpa* (cosmic cycle of time), all beings are merged into My *prakriti*, material nature; at the beginning of another *kalpa*, I send them forth again. (8) Activating My own *prakriti*, I project again and again this multitude of beings, helpless under the sway of my material nature. (9) But these actions do not bind Me, Arjuna, for I remain detached from them like one unconcerned. (10) With Me as overseer, *prakriti* produces the moving and unmoving universe. Because of this, Arjuna, the world revolves.

(11) Fools disregard Me as one clad in human form, not knowing my higher nature as the Supreme Lord of beings. (12) With vain hopes, vain actions, vain knowledge, and devoid of discrimination, they become deluded and possessed by a fiendish and demoniac temperament.

(13) But those noble souls, Arjuna, partaking of My divine nature, knowing Me to be the immutable source of beings, worship Me with unwavering mind. (14) Always glorifying Me, striving with firm resolve, honoring Me, they worship Me with devotion ever steadfast. (15) Others sacrificing in the form of knowledge worship Me, the all-faced, in various ways—as the one [without a second], as the distinct, or as manifold.

(16) I am the ritual, I am the sacrifice, I am the offering, I am the medicinal herb, I am the chanted hymn, I am also the clarified butter, I am the fire, and I am the oblation. (17) I am father, of this universe; the mother, the sustainer, the grandfather, the one to be known, the purifier, the sacred syllable Om, and also the Rig, Sāma and Yajur Vedas. (18) I am the goal, the maintainer, the Lord, the witness, the abode, the refuge, the friend, the origin, the dissolution, the substratum, the storehouse, and the imperishable seed. (19) I give heat; I withhold and send forth the rain; I am immortality as well as death; and I am existence and non-existence, Arjuna.

(20) Those who are versed in the three Vedas, being purified of sin (ignorance) by drinking the *soma* (intoxicating juice from a plant), worship Me by sacrifice and pray for passage to heaven. They reach the holy world of Indra (Lord of gods) and enjoy the heavenly pleasures of the gods. (21) After exhausting their merit by enjoying the vast sphere of heaven, they return to the mortal world. Thus, abiding by the injunctions of the Vedas, desiring enjoyments, they go and return. (22) Those persons who worship

Me alone, thinking of no other, who are ever devout, I provide what they lack and preserve what they already have. (23) Even those who worship other gods with faith, also worship Me, Arjuna, though not in the prescribed way. (24) I am the recipient and Lord of all sacrifices, but as they do not know Me in reality, they fall [return to the mortal world]. (25) Those who worship the gods go to the gods; those who worship ancestors go to the [world of] ancestors; those who worship elemental beings go to these beings; and those who worship Me come surely to Me.

(26) Whoever with devotion and a pure heart offers Me a leaf, a flower, a fruit or some water—that pious offering I accept. (27) Whatever you do, whatever you eat, whatever you offer in sacrifice, whatever you give away, whatever austerity you practice, do it as an offering to Me, Arjuna. (28) Thus shall you be free from the bondage of actions yielding good and bad results. Liberated, by means of this Yoga of renunciation, you shall come to Me.

(29) I am the same to all beings. There is none disliked or dear to Me. But those who worship me with devotion are in Me, and I am also in them. (30) Even if a most sinful man worships Me with undivided devotion, he must be regarded as righteous, for he has rightly resolved. (31) He soon becomes a pious soul and attains eternal peace. O Arjuna, know this to be certain that no devotee of mine perishes. (32) Any person who takes refuge in Me, even those [who might be considered] of inferior birth, such as women and those of lower classes [those without the opportunity for education and access to Scriptures], obtain the highest state. (33) Then how much more easily for the pure *brahmins* or devoted royal sages (*ksatriyas*) [those having the privileges of teachers, mentors, education and Scriptures]. Having obtained this impermanent and unhappy world, devote your self to Me.

(34) Fix your mind on Me, be devoted to Me, sacrifice to Me, and bow down to Me. Thus steadfast, with Me as your supreme aim, you will come and reach Me.

Chapter X
Divine Manifestations

As Krishna continues his talk with Arjuna, he describes how this manifested universe is the perceptible form of the imperceptible Supreme Self. Both the formless and the formful are one and the same. There is only one Supreme Source from which everything proceeds. No being, whether moving or unmoving, exists without the support of this Supreme Self.

Krishna explains that as we begin to incorporate this thinking into our lives—becoming steadfast and devoted—we receive the Yoga of discrimination which will lead us to the Supreme. With this power of discrimination, we realize the qualities of the Supreme dwelling within us as our sense of self. Krishna says, "I enter their *ātmabhāva*, inner feeling of self or being; and by the brilliant lamp of knowledge, destroy the darkness born of ignorance."

Arjuna asks Krishna to describe in detail His divine manifestations, so that he may understand them more. Krishna fulfills his wish, and then adds, "But what need is there, Arjuna, for this detailed knowledge? I stand supporting the whole universe with a single fragment of Myself. Whatever is the seed of all beings, that also I am, O Arjuna; there is no being, whether moving or unmoving, that can exist without Me."

Slokas

Śrī Krishna said: (1) O mighty-armed, to you who are gratified [by my speech], I shall describe one more excellent thing for your benefit. (2) My origin is not understood even by the multitude of gods, *devas*, or by the great seers, *rishis*; because in every way I am the source of the gods and great seers. (3) He who knows me as unborn and beginningless, as the great Lord of the worlds; he alone, among mortals, is not deluded and is liberated from all sins.

(4-5) Intellect, knowledge, non-delusion, forgiveness, truth, self-restraint, calmness, pleasure, pain, birth, death, fear and fearlessness, non-injury, equanimity, contentment, austerity, benevolence, fame and ill-fame—these different qualities arise from Me alone. (6) The seven great seers, the four ancient Manus, endowed with My power, were born of my mind; from them have come forth all the creatures in the world.

(7) He who knows in truth this manifold manifestation, splendor and Yoga power of Mine undoubtedly becomes established in the unshakeable Yoga. (8) I am the source of all; from Me everything proceeds. Thinking thus, the wise worship Me. (9) With their minds fixed on Me, with their life absorbed in Me, inspiring one another and always speaking of Me, they are contented and delighted. (10) To them, who are ever steadfast, worshipping Me with love, I give the Yoga of discrimination by which they come to Me. (11) Out of mere compassion for them, I enter their *ātmabhāva*, inner feeling of self or being; and by the brilliant lamp of knowledge, destroy the darkness born of ignorance.

Arjuna said: (12) You are the Supreme *Brahman*, the supreme abode, the supreme purifier, the eternal and luminous *puruṣa* (Self), the highest deity, the unborn, and the omnipresent. (13) All the seers have thus declared thee, as also the divine sages Nārada, Asita, Devala, and even Vyāsa. You also tell me the same thing. (14) All this which You speak to me, Krishna, I believe to be true. Indeed, neither the gods nor the demons, O Blessed One, know your manifestation. (15) Verily, You alone are the one, who know yourself—O Source of all beings, O God of gods, and Lord of the universe. (16) Please describe in detail to me all your divine manifestations, by which You pervade all these spheres and abide in them. (17) How may I know You, O Yogin, by continually meditating on You? And in what various aspects are You, O Lord, to be thought of by me? (18) Tell me again in detail, O Krishna, of your Yoga power and attributes, for I am not satiated in hearing your nectar-like words.

Śri Krishna said: (19) Very well, Arjuna, I shall now describe to you the most important of My divine manifestations, because there is no end to My expansion.

(20) I am the Self, Arjuna, which exists in the heart of all beings; I am the beginning, the middle and also the end of all beings. (21) I am *Vishnu* among the *Ādityas* (twelve months of year); I am the radiant sun among the luminaries; I am *Marichi* [foremost] among the *Maruts* (wind gods);

among the heavenly bodies, I am the moon; (22) I am the Sāma Veda among the Vedas; I am *Indra* (lord) among the gods; I am the mind among the senses; I am sentience within living beings.

(23) And among the eleven *Rudras* (cosmic functions), I am Śankara; I am [King] *Kubera* among the *Yakshas* and *Rakshasas* (acquirers and hoarders of wealth); I am the *Pāvaka* (fire) among the *Vasūs* (earth, water, fire, air, ether, moon, sun, and stars); [Mount] *Meru* among mountains; (24) And, among the household priests, Arjuna, know me to be the chief, *Brihaspati*; I am *Skanda* among army generals; among bodies of water, I am the ocean. (25) I am *Bhrigu* among the great *rishis* (seers); among speech, I am the one syllable *Om*; of *Yajñas* (sacrifices) I am *japa* (mental repetition); and among immovable things, the Himālyas. (26) Among all the trees, the *aśvattha* (fig tree); among the divine sages, *Nārada*; among *Gandharvas* (celestial beings), [King] *Citraratha*; and among *siddhas* (perfected souls), Kapila. (27) and the nectar-born *Ucchaisravas* among horses; *Airavata* among elephants; and the king among men.

(28) Among weapons I am the thunderbolt; among cows I am the wish-fulfilling cow *Kāmadhenu*; I am the progenitor, the god of love, *Kāma*; I am *Vāsuki* among the serpents; (29) I am *Ananta* of the *nāgas* (poisonous snakes); I am *Varuna* among the water deities; *Aryamā* among the ancestors; *Yama* (deity of death) among those who regulate. (30) Of the demons, *Prahlāda*; of measures I am *Kāla* (time); the lion among beasts; and *Garuda* (eagle) among birds. (31) Of purifiers I am the wind; I am *Rāma* among warriors; the alligator among water creatures; and the Ganges among the rivers.

(32) O Arjuna, I am the origin, the middle and the end of the entire creation; among science I am the science of Self; of those who debate I am logic. (33) I am the letter 'A' among the letters of the alphabet; and among compounds I am *dvandva* (coordinating conjunction); I alone am the inexhaustible time; I am the dispenser [of the fruits] of all actions having faces in all directions. (34) I am death, the destroyer of all; I am the origin of all things yet to be; of feminine qualities I am fame, prosperity, speech, memory, intellect, constancy, and forbearance.

(35) Similarly, among *Sāman* hymns I am the *Brhatsāman*; and among meters I am the *Gāyatrī*; I am *Margaśīrsa* (first) among months; and of seasons the flowery spring. (36) I am the gambling of the fraudulent; I am the splendor of splendid; I am victory, I am effort, I am the goodness of

the good. (37) Of the *Vrishnis* I am *Vāsudeva*; among the *Pāndavas* I am Arjuna; among the sages *Vyāsa*; and of the poets, *Uśana*. (38) I am the rod [of authority] of those who punish; I am statesmanship of those who seek victory; of secrets I am silence; and the wisdom of the wise.

(39) And whatever is the seed of all beings, that also I am, O Arjuna; there is no being, whether moving or unmoving, that can exist without Me. (40) There is no end of My divine manifestations, Arjuna, but this is a brief statement of the particulars of My divine powers or attributes. (41) Anything which is invested with power, glory, or splendor has come into existence from a fraction of My brilliance. (42) But what need is there, Arjuna, for this detailed knowledge? I stand supporting the whole universe with a single fragment of Myself.

Chapter XI
Vision of the Cosmic Form

Having heard from Krishna about His divine manifestations, Arjuna desires to see this cosmic form and requests to be given the vision of Krishna's universal form. Krishna explains that this form cannot be seen with eyes, but only with divine vision. He then grants Arjuna's request and opens his inner vision to show how this manifested universe is a projection of His cosmic form.

Arjuna sees our earth, its beings, and the whole universe contained within one Supreme entity. Everything is revealed as interconnected. Even though Krishna had explained the unity of all diverse manifestation, it was not until Arjuna received the vision that he could experience a deep understanding. Arjuna sees that everything is taking place within the Supreme's body. Both good and evil are present within. He sees that it is not within the power of the warrior to dispense death. Birth and death are cycles within a larger process; a warrior, such as himself, is merely an instrument of the cosmic movement. Arjuna is overwhelmed by the reality shown to him and requests that the vision be removed.

The vision of the one universal body that Krishna displays is similar to our own physical system. Within our body, when a virus enters and hijacks some of our cells, our immune system protects and fights. The immune system is a complex network of cells and chemicals whose mission is to protect us against foreign invasions. The cells have the ability to recognize a harmful entity and free the body of further trouble. We merely assist our body with proper nourishment and rest.

Many kinds of cells and hundreds of chemicals are smoothly coordinated within the immune system. The job of our immune system is to detect and eliminate a virus before it can embed itself and reproduce. If the virus creates further complications, the immune system continues to fight. The immune system with all of its warriors in the form of cells and chemicals is our *kṣatriya* class. Its members fight on our behalf to protect us and bring health to our physical system, which has been violated. The destruction of a virus might appear violent, but we do not mourn for the destroyed virus.

Within the body of the Supreme, there can be the attack of a virus or the complication of an infection. Then within this larger body, there is movement to overcome the evil. Krishna says that for the protection of the good and the destruction of evil, and for establishing righteousness, he takes birth in every age. There are many people who are committed to living a divine life who are part of the immune system of the Supreme body. Fighting is a natural response to disease within a system. To fight what is not serving society is not motivated by selfish interest or personal gain. This defensive action is applauded as performance of one's duty for the benefit of the whole.

Slokas

Arjuna said: (1) You have explained this profound mystery concerning the Self as a favor to me. With this understanding, my delusion has been dispelled. (2) I have heard from You in detail about the origin and dissolution of beings and also about Your inexhaustible greatness, O Krishna. (3) As You have described Yourself, O Supreme Lord, I wish to see Your divine form in that way, O Supreme Self. (4) If you think it is possible for me to see it, O Lord of Yoga, show me Your Imperishable Self.

Śrī Krishna said: (5) Behold My forms, Arjuna, by the hundreds upon thousands, manifold, divine, and of multi-colors and shapes. (6) Behold the *Ādityas*, the *Vasus*, the *Rudras*, the two *Aśvins*, and the *Maruts*. Behold these wonders never seen before, Arjuna. (7) Now, behold in this body of Mine, the whole universe centered in one—including everything moving and unmoving—and whatever else you desire to see Arjuna. (8) But you will not be able to see Me with your own eyes. Therefore, I am giving you divine sight; behold my lordly Yoga, divine power.

Sañjaya said to King Dhritarāshtra: (9) Having spoken thus, Krishna, the great Lord of Yoga, revealed to Arjuna His majestic supreme form. (10) With innumerable mouths and eyes, with numerous wondrous sights; [and] on it were shining ornaments of many kinds, [as well as] many celestial weapons. (11) That endless, all-facing, and resplendent Lord, wearing heavenly garlands and apparel and anointed with celestial perfumes. (12) If the effulgence of a thousand suns arose at once in the sky, that would be like the brilliance of this great *Ātman*, mighty being. (13) There in the body of the God of gods, Arjuna saw the entire universe established in one, with its manifold divisions. (14) Then Arjuna, being filled with amazement and with his hairs standing erect, bowed his head to the Lord, and with folded hands spoke.

Arjuna said: (15) O Lord, I see all the gods and diverse hosts of beings in Your body—*Brahma*, the lord [of gods], seated on a lotus and all the *rishis*, seers, and celestial serpents. (16) I see You, in forms endless on all sides, with countless arms, stomachs, mouths, and eyes; neither Your end, nor the middle, nor the beginning of Your cosmic form do I see, O Lord of the Universe. (17) I see You with crown, club and discus; a mass of radiance shining everywhere; [You] are very hard to look at blazing all round like a burning fire and with the immeasurable radiance of the sun.

(18) I think You are the Imperishable Supreme to be known, the ultimate support of this cosmos, the imperishable protector of eternal *dharma* (right action), and the Primal Being. (19) With infinite power, without beginning, middle or end, with endless arms, the sun and the moon being Your eyes, the burning fire Your mouth; I see You heating the whole universe with Your radiance. (20) This space between heaven and earth and all the quarters are filled by You alone; seeing this wonderful and terrible form, the three worlds tremble, O *Mahātman*, Great-soul One.

(21) Verily, the multitudes of gods enter into You; some terrified are praying with joined palms; bands of great seers and perfected ones, *siddhas*, praise you with splendid hymns. (22) Similarly, the *Rudras, Ādityas, Vasus, Sādhyas, Viśwas, Aśvins, Maruts, Usmapās,* hosts of *Gandharvas, Yakshas, Asuras* and *Siddhas*—are all gazing at You and they are amazed. (23) Seeing Your immeasurable form with many mouths and eyes, which has many arms, thighs and feet, with many stomachs and fearful with many tusks, O mighty-armed, the worlds are terrified and so am I.

(24) When I behold You touching the sky, brilliant, many colored, open-mouthed, with enormous, fiery eyes, my heart trembles with fear, O *Vishnu*, and I have lost both courage and peace. (25) And seeing these mouths of Yours, bearing many tusks aflame like the fires of cosmic dissolution, I know not the four quarters, nor do I find peace. Have mercy, O God of gods, abode of the universe. (26-27) All the sons of

Dhritarāshtra, with the hosts of kings of the earth, Bhīshma, Drona, and Karna, and also the most prominent warriors on our side, are rapidly entering into these terrible mouths with frightful tusks of Yours; some are seen with crushed heads and clinging between Your teeth.

(28) Just as the many torrents of rivers flow towards the ocean, so do these warriors from the world of humans enter Your flaming mouths. (29) As moths rush swiftly to their destruction into a blazing flame, so do these men rush swiftly into Your mouths to meet their destruction. (30) You lick up, devouring all the worlds on every side with Your flaming mouths. Filling the entire universe with effulgence Your fiery rays blaze forth, O *Vishnu*. (31) Tell me who You are, who have assumed this frightful form. I bow down to You, O God Supreme, have mercy. I desire to know You, O primal One. I do not understand this activity of Yours.

Śri Krishna said: (32) I am the mighty world-destroying time coming forth now to destroy the worlds. Even without any action of yours, none of these warriors standing in the various armies shall survive. (33) Therefore, stand up and attain glory. Conquer your enemies and enjoy a prosperous kingdom. They have already been slain by Me. Be merely an instrument, Arjuna. (34) Drona, Bhīshma, Jayadratha, Karna, and other warriors have been killed by Me. Do not be afraid, kill them. Fight! You are going to conquer the enemy in battle.

Sañjaya said: (35) Having heard the speech of Krishna, Arjuna, with joined palms, trembling, prostrating himself, overwhelmed with fear, bowed down and addressed Krishna in a choked voice.

Arjuna said: (36) Rightly it is, O Krishna, that the world delights and rejoices in Your praise; demons, terrified, flee in all directions, and the hosts of perfected ones bow to You. (37) And why should they not, O Great Soul, bow to You who is greater than all, the primal source of even the creator, *Brahma*. O Infinite Being, O Lord of gods, Abode of the universe; You are the Imperishable, the existent, the non-existent, and that which is Supreme and beyond both.

(38) You are the primal God, the ancient Spirit; the supreme support of this universe; You are the Knower and the Knowable; You are the supreme State. All this is pervaded by You, O One of Infinite forms. (39) You are *Vāyu, Yama, Agni, Varuna, Prajāpati* (progenitor of beings), and also the great grandfather. I bow down to You a thousand times. Again and again do I bow down before You. (40) I prostrate myself before You,

and behind You, and on all sides, O Soul of all. Infinite in power and immeasurable in strength, You pervade all, therefore You are all.

(41-42) Whatever I may have said disrespectfully to You by carelessness or familiarity, considering You as my friend and not recognizing Your greatness, Krishna; and whatever insult I may have offered to You in jest while at play, sporting, resting, or at meals when alone or in the presence of others—I implore You to forgive me, O immeasurable One. (43) You are the Father of this moveable and immoveable world, the object of its worship, the most venerable Guru. There is none equal to You in the three worlds. How then could there be another greater, O being of incomparable power? (44) Therefore, bowing down, prostrating the body, I implore Your mercy, O Lord. As a father forgives his son, a friend his friend, a lover his beloved, even so should You forgive me.

(45) Having seen that which no one has ever seen, I am delighted; and yet my mind trembles with fear. Show me Your previous form, O God of gods, have mercy. (46) I desire to see You as before, crowned, bearing a mace with discus in hand, in Your former form only, having four arms, O thousand-armed Cosmic Being.

Śri Krishna said: (47) By my grace, Arjuna, using my power of Yoga, I have shown to you this resplendent, universal, infinite, primal Cosmic Form, which no one else has ever seen. (48) Not by the study of the Vedas, nor by sacrifices, or by gifts, or by rituals, or by severe austerity can this form of Mine be seen in the world of men by any other than you, Arjuna. (49) Be not afraid or confused on seeing this terrible form of Mine; free from fear and with gladdened heart, behold again this former form of Mine.

Sañjaya said: (50) Having thus spoken, Krishna showed to Arjuna His own form. The Great Soul, assuming again a benign form, reassured Arjuna who had been terrified.

Arjuna said: (51) Having seen this gentle human form of Yours, Krishna, I am now composed and my mind is restored to normal.

Śri Krishna said: (52) It is very hard to behold this form of Mine, which you have seen. Even the gods long to behold this form. (53) It is not possible for any one to see Me, as you have seen Me, whether by the Vedas, or by austerity, or by charity, or by sacrifice. (54) Arjuna, only by single-minded devotion, is it possible to thus acquire knowledge of Me and be entered into Me. (55) Whoever does all actions for Me, who looks upon Me as the Supreme, who is devoted to Me, who is free from attachment, and free from enmity toward all beings, comes to Me, Arjuna.

Chapter XII
Devotion

In Chapter VII, Krishna related how all manifestation springs from one source. He revealed that there is an underlying unity of all diverse creation. Everything originates from the One and exists within the One, and yet the One, though all-pervading, is beyond all limitation. The One is infinite.

Krishna further explains that the Supreme Self is both the underlying unity and the diverse field of manifestation. The Supreme Self is the imperceptible and the perceptible, the immutable and the mutable. The imperceptible, unchanging aspect is realizable by reason, and the perceptible, mutable aspect is known through direct experience and observation. Realizing that there is only one imperishable Supreme Self which pervades all manifested worlds is known as *jñāna*, and understanding how diversity comes into existence and expresses out of one Supreme Source is known as *vjñāna*.

Tilak labels *jñāna* as Spiritual Knowledge and *vjñāna* as Empirical Knowledge. He explains that both are needed and supportive of the path of desireless action, which Krishna has described as Yoga. As our knowledge and discrimination become refined, the growth of devotion is a natural consequence. Devotion is accepting our role and purpose in this unfoldment and learning to participate fully within the divine manifestation. Both knowledge and devotion are essential to the path of Yoga.

The immutable, imperceptible *Brahman* was discussed in Chapter VIII. In Chapter IX Krishna explains the mystery of His all-pervasiveness and reminds us to fix our minds on Him, to be devoted to Him, to sacrifice to Him, and to bow down to Him. If we become steadfast, with Him (Supreme Self) as our supreme aim, then we may more easily reach the highest goal. In this way, Krishna emphasizes devotion. Chapters X and

XI provide descriptions of His many manifestations. And at the end of Chapter XI, Krishna advises Arjuna to perform all actions with devotion.

Now, Arjuna asks for clarification as to whether one should be devoted to the imperceptible or perceptible form of the Supreme Self.

Slokas

Arjuna said: (1) Who are the better knowers of Yoga [of desireless action]? Those devotees who are constantly steadfast and worship You, or those who worship the Imperishable, Unmanifest *Brahman*?

Śri Krishna said: (2) Those who have fixed their minds on Me, who are steadfast and integrated with Me, endowed with supreme faith, are the best in Yoga. (3-4) But those who worship the imperishable, the indefinable, the unmanifest, the omnipresent, the unthinkable, the immovable, and the eternal—having restrained all the senses, even-minded everywhere, engaged in the welfare of all beings—also come and reach Me. (5) Nevertheless, greater is their difficulty, whose minds are set on the unmanifest, for the goal of the unmanifest is very hard to be reached by embodied beings.

(6-7) But those who worship Me by dedicating all actions to Me, regarding Me as their Supreme, and meditate on Me with single-mindedness—such persons whose thoughts have entered into Me, I soon deliver from the ocean of birth and death, Arjuna. (8) [Therefore], keep your mind fixed on Me, set your intellect on Me, so that, hereafter, you will undoubtedly dwell in Me.

(9) If now you are unable to fix your mind steadily on Me, Arjuna, then seek to reach Me by practicing this Yoga again and again. (10) If you are unable to practice this [method], then be intent on doing actions for My sake; even by performing actions for My sake you will also attain success. (11) If you are not able to do even this, then taking refuge in Me and acting with self-restraint, abandon the fruits of action. (12) Because knowledge is superior to practice; meditation is superior to knowledge; abandoning the fruit of action is superior to meditation; and by this abandonment [of the expectation for a certain result] peace immediately follows.

(13-14) He, who hates no being, who is friendly and compassionate to all, from whom possessiveness and individuation have departed, who is even-minded in pain and pleasure, enduring, content, steady in meditation, self-restrained, is firm in his convictions, and who has dedicated his mind and intellect to Me—such a devotee of Mine is dear to Me.

(15) He, from whom the world has no cause to be frightened, who is not frightened by the world, who is free from joy, anger, fear and anxiety, is dear to Me. (16) He who is free from wants, who is pure, capable, unconcerned, untroubled, and who has relinquished expectation in undertakings—such devotee is dear to Me. (17) He who neither rejoices, nor hates, nor grieves, nor desires, renouncing good and evil, and is full of devotion is dear to Me. (18-19) He who is the same to friend and foe, and also in honor and dishonor, who is the same in cold and heat, and in pleasure and pain, who is free from attachment, indifferent to blame or praise, silent, contented with anything, having no place [the whole world is their home],[20] steady-minded, such a devoted person is dear to Me.

(20) They who follow this immortal *dharma* (law or doctrine) described above, endowed with faith, and who regard Me as the supreme goal, are exceedingly dear to Me.

---

[20] *Aniketa* means having no residence and is commonly translated as homeless, but it is not intended to mean that a person does not have a specific home or place to live, but that we find comfort in the whole world. Therefore, comfort is not dependent upon specific conditions or circumstances being met.

Chapter XIII
The Field and the Knower of the Field

In the previous chapter Krishna taught Arjuna that liberation can be attained by meditating on the unmanifest Imperishable, which is beyond description and omnipresent, while working for the welfare of others. However, according to Krishna, it is easier for embodied beings to gain the same release through devotion to the visible and perceptible form of Supreme (Godhead), by meditating on Him with single-mindedness and dedicating all actions to Him.

Arjuna has just experienced a magnificence that has left him trembling in fear. He perceived the diverse, manifested universe as contained in one, living organism—the body of the Supreme Lord. Krishna then explains that although this is a vision rarely seen by any being, even so, for those seeking liberation while living in the world, this idea is useful to hold in their minds: all manifestation is an expression of one Supreme Godhead.

Krishna went on to advise Arjuna that the person who has ill will toward no being, who is friendly and compassionate to all, from whom possessiveness and individuation have departed, who is even-minded in pain and pleasure, enduring, content, steady in meditation, self-restrained, is firm in his convictions, and who has a dedicated mind and intellect, is dear to Him. Krishna's purpose is to help Arjuna to hold this experience of oneness while bringing him back to his daily existence. Krishna's emphasis is devotion—holding the vision of the Supreme Lord—while performing action. Devotion supports unity, not divisiveness.

Now in Chapter XIII, Krishna resumes his description of *prakriti*. In Chapter III, He taught that all action takes place in nature, called *prakriti*, and is governed by its attributes or qualities. Here, He elaborates by explaining how the causal energy of nature projects into all forms and functions through its own attributes while the Self remains separate from this activity. This knowledge of the field and the knower of the field—*prakriti* and *purusha*—will help Arjuna to rise above possessiveness and individuation and remain fixed in Yoga—Unity. This understanding will enable him to work without doership, resting in the non-doer, even-minded above pleasure and pain, while performing desireless action.

The Self or soul is in fact separate from activity, yet as a result of egoism, we incorrectly believe ourselves to be the actor and doer. Also in Chapter III, Krishna explained that the egoistic tendency arises out of the quality of *rajas*, the restless, passionate attribute of nature. Once this egoistic self has been accepted as our real Self, we experience a sense of loss, and, prompted by a desire to overcome the loss, we mistakenly follow a course of action wherein, if desire is thwarted, we become angry. This cycle of misery envelops the soul, which leads to a loss of discrimination.

Patanjali, in the *Yoga Sutras*, elaborates on this cycle of misery, which he calls the *kleshas*. Egoism, or *asmita*—a cognitive blending of the qualities of nature with the qualities of Self—is the result of ignorance. The acceptance of the limited doer-ship of the ego as self produces a need for comparison, which engenders the duality of liking and disliking, of possessiveness and avoidance, and of pleasure and pain. These dualities further manifest as the jealousy, desire, anger, attachment, anxiety, and fear that disturb our equilibrium and peace.[21]

There are two words in Sanskrit, which describe how we experience the self—*aham* and *ahamkāra*. *Aham* is a pure sense of existence, completely and inseparably integrated with the Supreme Self. *Aham* emerges from the manifestion of the Supreme Self in the medium of the *chitta*, which is light-filled causal energy. Accepting the medium and its expressions in nature as the cause of our existence, results in a limited sense of self called *ahamkāra*. We need to understand and respect both experiences of the self in our lives.

The experience of *aham* is untouched by individuation and possessiveness. Chapter XIII describes *aham* as the knower of the field of all thoughts and forms of material nature. It is *purusha*—the witness, the knower, the seer, the non-doer. *Ahamkāra* is the active power of *prakriti*. It is part of the field of movement and change that is *prakriti*. It is the manifested form of our belief system. It is the doer, the performer of actions, and applier of effort for attaining eternal life.

---

21 *Yoga Sūtras* II/3-9.

In Chapter VII, Krishna states, "Earth, water, fire, air, ether, the mind (*manas*), intellect (*buddhi*) and individuation (*ahamkāra*)—thus my material nature is divided eightfold. This is my inferior nature. But know this as distinct from my higher nature, the life element (*jīvabhūtām*) by which this universe is maintained. Know that all beings have these two as the source of their birth." We all have a higher and lower nature, and it is important to understand both of these aspects of self—the knower of the field and the field.

Many versions of the *Gītā* open Chapter XIII with an unnumbered *sloka* in which Arjuna asks Krishna a question: "I wish to know about *prakriti* and *purusha*, the field and the knower of the field, knowledge and the knower of knowledge." In their commentary they explain that this question is included to set the stage for a new topic of discussion. I, however, do not agree that Arjuna is ready to pose a question at this juncture. Considering Arjuna's state of mind—being overwhelmed by the vision of the cosmic form of Godhead—it seems more reasonable that Krishna would gradually lead Arjuna from his highly sensitive state back to the battlefield. Arjuna need not ask any question. Krishna tells him, "The knowledge of the field and its Knower is deemed by Me as true knowledge. My devotee, understanding this, enters into My state of being." In other words, we attain the Supreme and are able to hold the vision and experience of the Supreme while living and acting in this world.

Slokas

Śri Krishna said: (1) Arjuna, this body is called *kshetra*, the field; he who knows it is call *kshetrajña*, the knower of the field, by those who know [truth]. (2) And know Me as the Knower (Self) in all fields (bodies). The knowledge of the field and its Knower is deemed by Me as true knowledge.

(3) Hear briefly from Me what the field is, what its properties are, what its modifications are, and whence they come; and who He (Knower of the field) is and what His powers are. (4) This has been sung by seers in many ways, in various distinctive Vedic hymns and also in well-reasoned and conclusive passages on *Brahman* in the Upanishads.

(5) The five primordial elements (ether, air, fire, water, and earth), *ahamkāra* (individuality), *buddhi* (intellect), *avyakta* (unmanifest nature), the ten senses and one (mind), and the five objects of senses (sound, touch,

form, taste, and smell). (6) Desire, hatred, pleasure, pain, the aggregate (body), intelligence, firmness—this briefly describes the field with its modifications.

(7-11) Humility, unpretentiousness, non-injury, patience, straight-forwardness, service of the teacher, purity, steadfastness, self-control, indifference towards the objects of senses, absence of egoism, reflection on the evil in birth, death, old age, disease, and pain, non-attachment, absence of clinging to son, wife, home and the like, and constant even-mindedness to all desirable and undesirable events, unwavering devotion to Me with single-minded Yoga, frequenting secluded places, disinclination to mingle in society, constant contemplation on the knowledge pertaining to the Self, and reflection for the attainment of the truth—this is declared to be knowledge, and what is contrary to it is ignorance.

(12) [Now] I will declare that which has to be known, knowing which one attains immortality; it is the beginningless, supreme *Brahman*, which is said to be neither existent nor non-existent. (13) With hands and feet everywhere, with eyes, heads and mouths on all sides, with ears everywhere—It pervades everything in this world. (14) Shining by the functions of the senses, yet without the senses; though It is untouched by anything, It supports everything; and devoid of the qualities (*gunas*), yet It experiences all the qualities. (15) Without and within all beings; the unmoving and also the moving; because of Its subtlety, It is incomprehensible; It is far and also it is near. (16) Undivided, yet It seems as if divided in all beings; It is to be known as the sustainer, devourer and source of all beings. (17) The light of all lights; it is said to be beyond darkness; It is knowledge, the object of knowledge, and that which is to be attained through knowledge. It is seated in the hearts of all.

(18) Thus the field, knowledge, and the object of knowledge have been briefly described. My devotee, understanding this, enters into My state of being.

(19) Know that *prakriti*, material nature, and *purusha*, self, are both eternal. Know that all evolutes (modifications) and the attributes, *gunas*, emerge out of *prakriti*. (20) *Prakriti* is said to be the cause for the activity of the body and the senses. [The presence of] *Purusha* is said to be the cause for experiencing pain or pleasure. (21) *Purusha* abiding in nature experiences the qualities born of nature; attachment to these qualities is

the cause of its birth in good and evil wombs. (22) The highest Self in this body is called the spectator, the consenter, the supporter, the experiencer, the great Lord, and the Supreme Self. (23) He who thus knows the *purusha* and *prakriti* together with the *gunas*, in whatever position he has in life, is never born again.

(24) Some persons perceive the Self within themselves by means of meditation; others by the Yoga of knowledge (Sāmkhya Yoga); and still others by the Yoga of action (Karma Yoga). (25) Others also, not knowing these means, worship as they have heard from others; they too go beyond death by their devotion to what they have heard.

(26) Remember, Arjuna, whatever moveable or immoveable form comes into existence is the result of the union between the field and the knower of the field. (27) He, who sees the Supreme Lord existing alike in all beings, the imperishable within the perishable, truly sees. (28) Realizing the same Lord equally present everywhere, that person escapes self-destruction and attains the supreme goal. (29) He, who sees that all actions are performed exclusively by *prakriti*, and that the Self is inactive (not the doer), sees indeed. (30) When a person sees the diversity of all beings as resting in the One, and understands [this] manifestation extends from That alone; then he attains *Brahman*.

(31) This imperishable Supreme Self is beginningless and without qualities; even though situated in the body, Arjuna, It does not act, nor is It tainted. (32) As the all-pervading *akāśa*, space, is not limited by anything because of its subtlety; so the Self, abiding in the body, is not limited [by the body]. (33) As the sun alone illumines this entire world, so does the knower of the field (Supreme Self) illumine the entire field, Arjuna.

(34) They who know, with the eye of knowledge, this distinction between the field and the knower of the field; and the deliverance of beings from the *prakriti*, they go to the Supreme.

Chapter XIV
Three *Gunas*

Nature, or *prakriti*, has three attributes called the *gunas*: *sattva*, *rajas* and *tamas*. The roots of the term *prakriti*, *pra*, *kr*, and *iti*, are found in the three *gunas*. *Sattva* is called *prakash*, luminous light. *Rajas* is *kriyā*, subtle movement. *Tamas* is *sthiti*, stability. The three *gunas* combined are *pra-kr-iti*, and have the qualities of light, movement and stability.

Vedanta describes this universe as a projection of *māyā*. Sāmkhya states the universe is a projection of *prakriti*, nature. Both *māyā* and *prakriti* refer to the root cause of this material universe. The three *gunas*, or attributes, are either a projection of *māyā* or exist as intrinsic qualities of *prakriti*. A significant difference between the philosophies is that Vedanta considers *māyā* to be the divine power of the Supreme Lord while Sāmkhya considers *prakriti* as a separate power, along with *purusha*.

Although Nature is one, it exists in four stages: formless, causal, subtle, and gross, and the three *gunas* exist together at every stage. These three attributes are in balance in the formless state, and they become the means by which Nature transforms into causal, subtle and gross forms. *Prakriti* is the one root cause of all phenomena, all manifestation, and all activity. Form is nothing more than the combined elements of earth, water, fire, air and space, and the resultant diversity of forms is an expression of different combinations of the three attributes. The whole universe and the experience of every person's life is the result of these three *gunas*.

The three *gunas* are the qualities of nature and are ever present with nature. Just as fire does not exist without heat and light; nature does not exist without these three attributes. All three *gunas* are responsible for the constant transformations of nature. They cannot be separated; they reside together and are dependent on each other. There is no question as to whether all three are operating at any moment. It is always a matter of which *guna* is dominant.

The *Sāmkhya Karika* provides the example of an oil lamp as a demonstration of how independent objects with opposing qualities work together to create light.[22] In this example, the stable wick is *tamas*; oil is *rajas* and the brilliant fire is *sattva*. Just as fire, wick and oil together compose a lamp, creating light that is useful for others, in the same way these three different *gunas* work together and become useful in all human endeavors, giving light, inspiration and stability.

The *gunas* are beyond perception, so we know them only by their effects. The quality of our thoughts is determined by the dominant *guna*. *Sattva* is experienced as pleasure and attraction; *rajas* as pain and rejection; and *tamas* as indifference and holding. With the quality of attraction, *sattva* gives light; with rejection, *rajas* brings movement; and with holding or restraining, *tamas* offers stability.

When, with an unclouded intellect, we begin to understand cause and effect, we realize the indwelling Self as the observer and knower of all projection. This observer is beyond Nature because the observer can observe all of Nature. This Knower is our real self. Gradually, with discrimination, we become established in the Knower or indweller that is above all states of the *gunas*. The Self is separate from energy; the Self is existence, intelligence, and bliss.

Slokas

Śri Krishna said: (1) I shall further declare that highest knowledge, the best of all knowledge, knowing which all the sages have gone from this world to the highest state. (2) They who, having taken refuge in this knowledge, have attained a state of unity with Me, are neither born at the time of creation, nor are they disturbed at the time of dissolution.

(3) Arjuna, My womb is the great *Brahman* (*prakriti*), in it I place the seed. From that is the origin of all beings. (4) Whatever forms are produced in any wombs whatsoever, *prakriti* is their womb and I am the seed-giving Father.

(5) The attributes, *gunas*—*sattva*, *rajas* and *tamas*—which arise from *prakriti* bind the immutable embodied one to the body, Arjuna. (6) Of these, *sattva*, because it is pure, is luminous and not obstructive. It binds by attachment to pleasure and to knowledge, Arjuna. (7) Know that *rajas*

---

[22] Sāmkhya Karika XIII.

is characterized by passion springing from thirst and attachment. It binds the embodied one by attachment to action. (8) But know *tamas* is born of ignorance, deluding all embodied beings; it binds with heedlessness, indolence and sleep. (9) *Sattva* generates attachment to pleasure, *rajas* to action, while *tamas* shrouds knowledge and spawns negligence, Arjuna.

(10) *Sattva* asserts itself by prevailing over *rajas* and *tamas*; *rajas* by prevailing over *sattva* and *tamas*, likewise *tamas* by prevailing over *sattva* and *rajas*. (11) When the light of knowledge shines through all the gateways of the body (senses), then it may be known that *sattva* is dominant. (12) Greed, inclination towards action, undertaking of action, unrest, longing—these arise, Arjuna, when *rajas* is dominant. (13) Darkness, inertness, heedlessness and confusion arise when *tamas* prevails, Arjuna.

(14) If the embodied one meets death when *sattva* is predominant, then he proceeds to the pure worlds of those who know the highest [truth]. (15) Meeting with death when *rajas* is prevalent, one takes birth among those who are engrossed in action. Likewise, one who dies when *tamas* is dominant is born in the wombs of beings lacking in intelligence.

(16) The fruit of good action, they say, is *sāttvic* and pure; verily the fruit of *rājasic* action is pain; and ignorance is the fruit of *tāmasic* activity. (17) Wisdom arises from *sattva*, and from *rajas* greed; negligence, confusion and indeed ignorance arise from *tamas*. (18) Those established in *sattva* go upwards (heavenly spheres); the *rājasic* remain in the middle (human life); and those abiding in *tāmasic* tendencies go downwards (lower states of human life, animals, birds, insects, and into immovable objects).

(19) When the seer realizes that there is no agent of action other than the *gunas*, and knows that which is higher than the qualities, he attains my state of being. (20) The embodied one, having gone beyond these three *gunas* from which the body evolved, is freed from birth, death, old age and sorrow and attains immortality.

Arjuna said: (21) O Lord, what are the marks of a man who has transcended these three *gunas*? What is his conduct? And how does he go beyond these three qualities?

Śri Krishna said: (22) Arjuna, he who does not hate illumination (seeing things as they are), activity, or delusion when present, nor longs for them when they are absent. (23) He sits like one unconcerned, undisturbed by the *gunas*; who remains steady and does not waver, knowing that the qualities are performing [their respective] functions; (24)

who is balanced in pleasure and pain; who is Self-abiding; who regards earth, stone, and gold alike; looks upon the agreeable and disagreeable the same; who is steadfast; and who regards censure and praise the same (other's opinion); (25) to whom honor and dishonor are equal; who is impartial towards friend or foe; and who has relinquished all undertakings—he is said to have gone beyond the *gunas*.

(26) And he who serves Me with unswerving devotion, having gone beyond the *gunas*, is fit for becoming one with *Brahman*. (27) For I am the abode of *Brahman*—the immortal and imperishable—the eternal dharma and abode of absolute bliss.

Chapter XV
Purushottama (Highest Self)

The word *Brahman* is derived from the root *brinh*, to expand. This indicates two qualities: the material of expansion and the efficient cause of expansion. Both qualities belong to *Brahman*. "Just as a spider produces a web from within itself, and then dwells in its web; supreme *Brahman* projects the universe from within itself, and then enters and resides in it."[23] *Brahman* is the source of the universe and pervades the universe.

Chapter XV describes this Supreme Source as *Purushottama*, the Highest Self. The Supreme Self has two aspects—the *ksara*, the perishable, and the *aksara*, the imperishable. The perishable, known as the field, consists of all beings, while the unchanging, the knower of the field, is called the imperishable. In the Vedas, this Highest Self is known as *Paramātman*, Supreme Self. The eternal Lord (*Īsvara*), the Supreme Self, pervades the three worlds and supports them. In Chapter XV, Krishna says, "As I am beyond the perishable and am even above the imperishable, therefore, I am known in the world as *Purushottama*, the Highest Self."

Slokas

Śri Krishna said: (1) They speak of the indestructible *asvattha* tree having its roots above and branches below. Its leaves are the Vedas. He who knows it knows the Vedas. (2) Its branches, nourished by the *gunas*, spread above and below; above forming buds—the objects of the senses—and below secondary roots, which take hold in the human world and initiate action.

(3-4) Its form is not perceived here in this world—neither its end, nor its beginning, nor its support. Having cut asunder this firm-rooted tree with the strong axe of non-attachment; one should seek that goal from

---

[23] *Mundaka Upanishad* I.1.7.

which, having attained, no one returns. Seek refuge in that primal *Purusha* (Self), from which this ancient [creative] activity streamed forth.

(5) Free from pride and delusion, victorious over the evils of attachment, constantly engrossed in the Eternal Self, those who are desireless and free from the pairs of opposites, known as pleasure and pain, such non-deluded reach that imperishable goal. (6) That supreme abode of Mine, to which having gone, no one returns—the sun does not illuminate, nor the moon, nor fire.

(7) Merely a fragment of Myself becomes the eternal *jīvabhūta*, individual life element, in the world of the living, and draws [to itself] the senses with mind as the sixth that exist in *prakriti*, nature. (8) When this lord (*jīvabhūta*) acquires a body and when he departs it, he takes these senses and mind and goes, as the wind carries the scents from their sources. (9) Presiding over the ear, the eye, the touch, the taste, and the smell, and also the mind, he experiences the objects of the senses. (10) The deluded do not perceive that, which departs, stays, and enjoys, because of being united with the *gunas*, but those with the eye of knowledge see him. (11) The *yogis*, who strive, realize him established in themselves, but though striving, the unrefined and unintelligent see him not.

(12) That brilliance in the sun, which illumines the whole world; that which is in the moon and in the fire—know that brilliance to be Mine. (13) Entering the earth I support all beings with My energy, and becoming the watery moon I nourish all plants. (14) Abiding in the body of living beings as the digestive fire, and being united with the *prāna*, inward, and the *apāna*, outward, breaths, I digest the four kinds of food [that which is chewed, sucked, licked, and drunk]. (15) And I am seated in the hearts of all; memory, knowledge, as well as their loss is My doing; I am That which is to be known by all the Vedas; I am the author of Vedānta, and I am the knower of the Vedas.

(16) There are two *purushas* (entities) in this sphere—the *ksara*, perishable, and the *aksara*, imperishable. The perishable is all beings and the unchanging, *kūtastha*, is called the imperishable (*kūta* means root—*Īsvara* is the root of all beings). (17) But the Highest Self is another. It is known as *Paramātman*, Supreme Self, in all the Vedas, who, pervades the three worlds as the eternal Lord (*Īsvara*), and supports them. (18) As I am

beyond the perishable and am even above the imperishable, therefore, I am known in the world as *Purushottama*, Highest Self.

(19) He who is free from delusion, thus knows Me as the Highest Self, knowing all, worships Me with his whole being, Arjuna. (20) Thus, this most secret science has been taught by Me, O sinless one. By understanding this, a person becomes a knower and has done all that ought to be done.

Chapter XVI
Divine and Demoniac

Within Arjuna's vision of the Cosmic Form, hosts of divine beings honor and bow to the Supreme Lord, and terrified demons flee in all directions. Arjuna's enemies, the sons of Dhritarāshtra, with the hosts of kings and prominent warriors are crushed in terrible and frightful mouths. "As moths rush swiftly to their destruction into a blazing flame, so do these men rush swiftly into your mouths to meet their destruction." Arjuna saw the Lord as the mighty world-destroying Time. Krishna says, "Even without any action of yours, none of these warriors standing in the various armies shall survive. They have already been slain by Me. Be merely an instrument, Arjuna."

Now, Krishna proceeds to explain the characteristics of both divine and demoniac beings. *Āsura* is the word used to signify the demoniac. In early scriptures, *āsuras* were beings who sought personal power while denying the existence of any higher power. They were concerned only with their own welfare, engaging in sensual enjoyment, and delighting in the domination of others and the environment. They were constantly at odds with deities and society. Here, Krishna explains how those individuals who develop demoniac qualities harm others and themselves, which leads to their own inevitable downfall.

Krishna continues to shed light on Arjuna's misconception regarding his duty as a *kṣatriya*, so that he may be able to act on the battlefield. He is not the cause of another's destruction. For the evil-minded, time alone will precipitate their destruction.

Slokas

Śri Krishna said: (1-3) Fearlessness, purity of heart, steadfastness in knowledge and Yoga, generosity, control of the senses, sacrifice, study of the scriptures, austerity, straightforwardness, non-injury, truth, absence of anger, renunciation of fruit or expectation, tranquility, non-slandering,

88

compassion for all beings, non-covetousness, gentleness, modesty, absence of fickleness, vigor, forgiveness, fortitude, purity, non-hatred, absence of pride—these are acquired by persons, who are born to godlike endowments, Arjuna.

(4) Hypocrisy, arrogance, self-conceit, anger, cruelty, and ignorance are acquired by those who are born in the *āsurī*, ungodly, endowment. (5) The divine qualities are deemed to lead to liberation and the demoniac to bondage. Grieve not, Arjuna, you are born to a divine destiny.

(6) There are two types of beings in this world—*daiva*, divine, and *āsura*, power-seekers called demoniacal. The divine have been described at length; hear from Me, Arjuna, about the demoniacal. (7) The persons with demoniac qualities do not know what should be done, or what should be refrained from; neither is purity found in them, nor good conduct, nor truth. (8) They say, 'The universe is unreal, without support, existing without a God. What can be the object of it, if not enjoying the objects of sense by humans?'

(9) Holding this view, these feeble-minded, malicious, lost souls perform cruel actions, and rise as enemies of the world causing its destruction. (10) Filled with insatiable sensual desires, full of hypocrisy, arrogance, and pride, accepting false notions through delusion, they act with selfish motives. (11-12) Beset with immeasurable anxiety ending only with death, regarding gratification of desires as the highest end, firmly believing that that is everything; bound by a hundred snares of hope, given over to lust and anger, they strive unjustly to gather wealth for the gratification of their desires.

(13) [They think], this I have gained today, and this desire I shall attain; this wealth is mine, and that [wealth] will become mine. (14) That enemy has been slain by me, and I shall destroy others; I am the lord, I am the enjoyer, I am successful, powerful, and happy. (15) I am wealthy and high-born; who else is equal to me? I shall sacrifice, I shall give, I will rejoice. Thus, they are deluded by ignorance.

(16) Led astray by many imaginings, entangled in a net of confusion, addicted to sensual enjoyment, they fall into a foul hell. (17) Self-conceited, haughty, filled with the pride and intoxication of wealth, they perform nominal sacrifices in name only, with hypocrisy and not according to scriptural injunctions. (18) Possessed of egoism, power, insolence, lust and wrath, these malicious people hate Me in their own

bodies and those of others. (19) These malicious and cruel evil-doers, the lowest among men, I constantly hurl into the wombs of the demoniac. (20) Arjuna, these foolish persons, taking birth in demoniac wombs, never come to Me, and ultimately reach the lowest of low conditions.

(21) The gateway to hell is three-fold—desire, anger, and greed. They destroy the self. Therefore, one should abandon these three. (22) Arjuna, when a person escapes from these three gates of darkness, he begins to act in a way which is beneficial to him, and ultimately reaches the highest state. (23) He, who acts under the impulse of desire, casting aside the guidance of scriptures, does not attain perfection, happiness, or the highest goal. (24) Therefore, let the scripture be your authority in determining what ought to be done and what ought not to be done. Knowing the scriptural injunction prescribed, you should perform action in this world.

Chapter XVII
Threefold Faith

Having heard the descriptions of the divine and the demoniac, Arjuna now asks why these differences exist. He poses the question to Krishna: "What is the position of those who perform sacrifice, (perform action) without observing the scriptures, but are filled with faith [or determination to act]." In other words, how did these beings become established in their divergent positions? Krishna responds, "The faith of embodied beings is of three kinds—*sāttvic*, *rājasic*, and *tāmasic*—born out of their innate nature...whatever faith he is, that verily he is."

Prakriti, nature, is unmanifest, infinite and one, but produces finite and diverse things. Unmanifest Nature produces all of the effects by the combination and modification of the three attributes, the *gunas*. These three *gunas* are responsible for diversity. The *Samkhya Karika* compares nature to water as a way of explaining how one Nature produces so many different effects.[24]

In Swami Bawra's commentary on this verse, he says:

> We can understand this by considering that water falling from the clouds nourishes many kinds of seeds and produces different kinds of tastes from different plants. The same water produces different effects. The different tastes within plant life are created by the many abodes of seeds nourished by rain. When water nourishes sugar cane plants they become sweet. If it nourishes a chili plant, the fruit is hot. A lemon tree produces a bitter taste. Water produces different tastes, not because of its own quality, but because of the quality of the seed and plant that it nourishes. The medium is responsible for the changing taste, not water, which is the same in each abode.

---

[24] *Sāmkhya Karika* XVI.

In the same way, Nature is one, but there are different kinds of abodes or media which produce diversity. There are media for plants, trees, reptiles, insects, birds, animals, and human beings. Even, within one branch of beings there is much diversity such as different breeds of cows. This differentiation is the result of the three *gunas,* which reside in various abodes and create diversity.

What is this abode or medium of Nature, which acts like a seed producing diversity? This is an important philosophical question. This abode or medium is given many different names. In the Upanishads the medium is called *sattva* or *brahma chakra;* Yoga calls this medium *chitta;* and Sāmkhya uses *mahat* or intellect. These terms indicate a medium that adopts and manifests consciousness. This medium is the first projection of Nature or energy and it has an individual quality. It is because of this medium that our sense of existence or soul seems contained, limited or individual, just as walls seem to limit space and create individual spaces. When this medium is enlivened with spirit or consciousness, it is called *purusha,* indweller, or *jivātma,* individual soul, because of the individual quality of the medium and not because of any limitation of the Knower or Spirit.

In our modern world, we have the example of a computer chip. A very small chip, made from a tiny piece of silicon, is able to receive and process a vast number of instructions. The abode of *sattva* is even smaller than a computer chip, yet it adopts and manifests infinity in the form of our own self. The medium collects and holds millions of impressions from our previous lives. These impressions are the cause of our current physical form, our abilities, and evolutionary development. They determine the span of our lives and structure the results we receive from previous actions. In other words, these impressions are the particular characteristics of the three attributes and are responsible for diversity.

Therefore, it is this abode that is responsible for diversity or individuation. There are numerous media, countless *chittas* or abodes, with different combinations of the three attributes projected from one unmanifest Nature. So, the three attributes are responsible for diversity. One infinite Nature or energy works in the form of three attributes. And according to the particular characteristics of the *gunas* held in the abode, diverse forms appear.[25]

Krishna explains that the faith of every person is according to their *sattvānarūpā*. *Sattva* indicates the first projection of *prakriti*. In Chapter XV, Krishna says, "Merely a fragment of Myself, becomes the eternal *jīvabhūta*." This individual life element is our causal form, which becomes colored or enveloped, "as it draws to itself the senses and mind that exist in *prakriti*, nature. When this life element acquires a body and when it departs, it takes the senses and mind and goes, as the wind carries the scents from their sources."

Our journey towards realization and liberation continues over lifetimes. The experiences we encounter are stored as impressions, *samskaras*, which surround our causal medium and form our discriminative ability, the intellect. The impressions become the basis for our reasoning or our beliefs regarding how we may attain happiness. Our beliefs appear in patterns of behavior or tendencies of liking and disliking—*ahamkara*. Egoism is the form or *rūpā* of our impressions surrounding the life element. It is the form of our innate nature and inherent disposition. All of this activity is the result of the three *gunas* modifying and acting.

The human condition is dominated by the passion of *rajas*, alternating between the clarity of *sattva* and the dullness of *tamas*. Dull people have both *sattva* and *rajas*, but they live under the constraints of *tamas*. In a person of knowledge, *sattva* prevails with the properties of *rajas* and *tamas* expressing under the guidance of a *sāttvic* intellect.

Individuality starts with the causal medium, and the quality of our individual life is determined by the state of our intellect. If our intellect is overwhelmed by *rajas* and *tamas*, we will find life difficult. When greed, passion, temptation or ignorance prevail, we experience instability, agitation, frustration, fatigue, sluggishness, and hopelessness. By contrast, when *sattva* prevails in the intellect, we feel comfortable and good. Krishna says, "Man consists of faith—whatever faith he is, that verily he is."

---

[25] See *Sāmkhya Kārikā with Guadapadacarya Bhāsya*, commentary by Brahmrishi Vishvatma Bawra, compiled and edited by William Milcetich, Brahmrishi Yoga Publications, 2012.

Slokas

Arjuna said: (1) O Krishna, what is the position of those who perform sacrifice without observing the Scriptural methods, but are filled with *śraddhā*, faith? Is it *sattva, rajas* or *tamas*?

Śri Krishna said: (2) The faith of embodied beings is of three kinds—*sāttvic, rājasic,* and *tāmasic*—born out of their innate nature. Now listen about it. (3) Faith is in accord with the inherent disposition of each, Arjuna. Man consists of faith—whatever faith he is, that verily he is. (4) The *sāttvic* worship the gods; the *rājasic* worship wealth and power, and the *tāmasic* worship [disembodied] spirits and nature beings. (5-6) Those men who undergo intense austerities not enjoined by the scriptures, being imbued with hypocrisy and egoism, and prompted by the force of lust and passion, these undiscriminating men, torturing all the elements in the body and Me also, who dwell within the body—know them to be demoniacal in their resolves.

(7) Also, the food preferred by all is of three kinds. So are the sacrifices, austerities and gifts. Hear now the distinction between them. (8) The foods that augment vitality, energy, vigor, health, joy and cheerfulness, which are savory, rich in oil, substantial and agreeable to the stomach are dear to *sāttvic* people. (9) Foods that are bitter, sour, too salty, exceedingly hot, pungent, dry and irritating are liked by the *rājasic* and are productive of pain, misery and disease. (10) That which is stale, tasteless, putrid, rotten, and impure is the food liked by the *tāmasic.*

(11) The sacrifice, performed by those desiring no fruit and with a firm understanding that it is a duty as enjoined by scriptures, is *sāttvic.* (12) But that sacrifice which is performed in expectation of a reward or for self-glorification, Arjuna, know that to be *rājasic.* (13) And that sacrifice performed without consideration of scriptures, in which no food is distributed, which is devoid of *mantras*, gifts, and faith, is said to be *tāmasic.*

(14) Worship of the gods, the twice-born, teachers, and the wise; purity, straight-forwardness, celibacy, and non-injury are called austerities of the body. (15) Speech which causes no pain, which is truthful, pleasant and beneficial, and also the practice of recitation of sacred texts are called austerities of speech. (16) Peace of mind, gentleness, silence, self-restraint, and purity of disposition—these are called austerities of mind.

(17) This threefold austerity practiced by steadfast men with utmost faith who are not desirous of fruits are regarded as *sāttvic*. (18) That austerity which is ostensibly practiced with the intent of gaining respect, honor, and reverence is here said to be *rājasic*—unsteady and impermanent. (19) That austerity practiced with a foolish obstinacy, with self-torture or for the purpose of destroying another, is declared to be *tāmasic*.

(20) The gift given to one who does nothing in return, with the feeling that it is one's duty to help, and which is given at the right place and time and to a worthy person, that gift is held to be *sāttvic* (21) But that gift that is given grudgingly, or in consideration for something received or in expectation of future reward is called *rājasic*. (22) And that gift, which is made to an improper place or at the wrong time, or to unworthy persons, without regard or with disdain, that is declared to be *tāmasic*.

(23) *Om tat sat*—thus *Brahman* is denoted by this threefold expression. By this the *brāhmanas*, the Vedas, and the sacrifices were created in ancient times. (24) Therefore, acts of sacrifice, giving, and austerity always begin by uttering the syllable *Om*, as prescribed in the scriptures, by the followers of the Vedas. (25) Uttering *tat*, the seekers of liberation, perform acts of sacrifice, austerity, and giving without aiming at fruits (specific results). (26) *Sat* is used to signify reality and goodness; and also, *sat* is used for an auspicious act Arjuna.

(27) Steadfastness in sacrifice, austerity, and giving is also called *sat*, and action related to these (or for the sake of the Supreme) is also called *sat*. (28) Whatever is sacrificed, given or performed and whatever austerity is practiced without faith is called *asat*, Arjuna. It has no value here or in the hereafter.

Chapter XVIII
Liberation through Renunciation

Reiterating his dilemma of whether or not to act, Arjuna now requests that Krishna clarify the difference between renunciation (*sannyāsa*) and abandonment (*tyāga*), but he couches this final concern within a cultural context. In regard to action, do the two terms renunciation and abandonment ultimately have the same meaning?

Krishna responds with the accepted interpretation of these terms: "The sages hold that *sannyāsa* is the giving up of all works motivated by desire. The wise declare *tyāga* to be the abandonment of the fruits of all works. Some sages say that all actions should be given up as evil; others declare that works such as sacrifices, gifts and austerities should not be given up."

Krishna continues, "Listen to my decision, O Arjuna. The acts of sacrifice, gifts and austerities should not be relinquished; they should be performed for they are the means of purification for the wise. It is my final view that these acts should be done with relinquishment of attachment and the fruits thereof. Abandonment of these through delusion will lead to one's downfall. It is impossible for one who bears a body to abandon actions entirely. But he who gives up the fruits of works is wise."

Tyāga is physical isolation from the objects of temptation, whereas renunciation is the cessation of the expectation that we will gain happiness from external attachments. Renunciation is detachment, *vairāgya*, literally the absence of *rāga*, attachment. *Rāga* is the attraction or attachment to situations, people and objects that give us pleasure. Detachment occurs when we stop expecting happiness from people, places and things. A person who leaves society and follows an austere life may cling to dreams of external fulfillment. True detachment may be maintained while living among the abundance of life.

Krishna emphasizes relinquishing the fruit of action in the light of knowledge, rather than shutting out the world. Our renunciation is not affected by the presence or absence of external objects unless we place value on the experience. Desire creates temporary feelings of joy when we obtain that which we desire and feeling of loss when our cravings are unfulfilled. These emotions spring from our desires and not from our needs. A need is a requirement of life and must be fulfilled. When we analyze worldly experiences and external objects, we can determine their actual value for us.

Chapter XVIII is a summary of Krishna's teaching on the Yoga of Action—desireless action. We are bound to act, but our reason and our free will that motivate our action are influenced by the three *gunas*. Whether by the light of sattva, the passion of rajas, or the by heedless quality of tamas, our motivation is embedded with the qualities of nature. Krishna says, "There is no being, either on earth or even among the gods in heaven, who is free from these three *gunas* of *prakriti*." After affirming the need to act, He describes how distinctions arise as a result of the predominance of one of the three *gunas*. He explains how these qualities appear as characteristics forming our knowledge, motivating our action, influencing the doer, the *ahamkara*, and tainting our reasoning. These combine to produce our suffering, our experience of happiness, or our freedom.

Our skills and abilities are structured by the *gunas*, and these inherent dispositions form our means to help society. We all have abilities, which we continue to cultivate during our lives. Krishna says that person who is engrossed in the performance of action while acting skillfully attains perfection. Gaining social status is in no way necessary for attaining spiritual perfection: "When a man performs the action which befalls him, while worshipping That from whom all beings have evolved and by whom all this is pervaded, he attains perfection."

Swami Bawra summarizes this Yoga of Action described in the *Bhagavad Gītā* as follows:

> The path of wisdom with love teaches that all of creation is a manifestation of the Supreme Lord. Nature is His divine power and has no separate existence or movement without His divine light and will. Everything that has a name and takes form is an expression of the Supreme Cause and is inseparably connected

with the divine. We are taught to love all, because all beings are manifestations of the divine. The practitioner of Yoga devotes all instruments, abilities, and strength to the service of all beings, because all beings are manifest forms of one Supreme Source.

We all share the same source of life, and we receive our life energy from this source. Although the Supreme Source is beyond our vision and perception, we can realize that it exists and we can approach it. The Supreme enlightens our medium, life element, with divine light and manifests as our life energy or *prāna*. This life energy is called soul and appears in our heart[26] as love.

Love is eternal, but when love becomes attached to worldly objects it loses its purity and becomes desire. When love is attached to sexuality, it expresses as passion or lust. With any hindrance, it appears as anger. All emotions are variations of this love. But love is not for worldly objects; it is for devotion. When our love is inspired by devotion, it becomes pure and unselfish and is more nourishing and helpful to the people in our lives.

We can devote our love to any form of divinity. In the beginning there is no need to fix our mind on the Supreme Lord. It is difficult to focus on something that is unknown to us. We can begin by making our mind one-pointed on whatever is dear to us, as Patanjali advises.[27] This practice purifies the mind. He also suggests focusing the mind on a person who is perfectly detached.[28] There is one valuable and intimate focus of the mind we all share: our breath. Breath is life.

When we relate our mind with breath, then thought and breath together lead us to our source. Each and every being receives life energy from this Supreme Source in the form of breath. As we realize our unity with this divine source, we experience divine love, and divine love compels us to serve the divinity manifesting in all beings. Pure love is desireless, and desireless love motivates non-binding actions.

---

[26] Philosophically, heart does not mean the physical heart. In Sanskrit, this place is indicated by the word *hridhayam*. It is the center that initiates the receiving and discharging of breath and is the medium that receives the light of consciousness.
[27] *Yoga Sūtras* I/35.
[28] *Yoga Sūtras* I/37.

The practitioner of Yoga acts without bondage because all actions are for divinity.[29] The work of the body, thoughts and speech are related with divine power. The *yogi* willingly dedicates all actions to divinity and benefits all beings. Practicing in this way, our entire being is aligned with divinity in every moment. Krishna tells, "Both renunciation with knowledge and the Yoga of action lead to incomparable bliss. Yoga of action is superior."[30]

All that we use is a gift of divinity. All that we do is for divinity. All that we see belongs to divinity. Divinity is the root of everything. We are only the medium for divinity to engage with this manifestation. All that exists comes from one Supreme Cause, exists to serve the Supreme Cause, and returns to the Supreme Cause. On this path, we realize divine unity in diversity and we gain emancipation.[31]

Krishna concludes by saying to Arjuna, "Thus the knowledge, the mystery of mysteries, has been declared to you by Me—reflect on it fully and do what you think best." Knowledge may be provided, but the choice to apply it rests with us. We have been given the necessary means to attain eternal happiness, as well as the free will to choose which action we will take. We can hear and read about this Supreme Knowledge, but it is up to us to reflect on it and implement it.

Arjuna chooses to act stating, "My delusion is destroyed. I have regained my memory through Your grace, Krishna. I am now free from doubts. I shall act according to Your word."

Slokas

Arjuna said: (1) I wish to know the truth about *sannyāsa*, renunciation, and *tyāga*, abandonment, respectively, O Krishna.

Śri Krishna said: (2) The sages hold that *sannyāsa* is the giving up of all desire-prompted actions. The wise declare *tyāga* to be the abandonment of the fruits of all works.

(3) Some sages say that all actions should be given up as evil; others declare that works such as sacrifices, gifts and austerities should not be

---

[29] *Bhagavad Gītā* V/2.

[30] *Bhagavad Gītā* V/2.

[31] *Yoga in Action*, Brahmrishi Vishvatma Bawra, Brahmrishi Yoga Publications, 2010.

given up. (4) Listen to my decision, Arjuna, about abandonment; abandonment is declared to be of three kinds. (5) The acts of sacrifice, gifts and austerities should not be relinquished, but should be performed; for sacrifices, gifts and austerities are the means of purification for the wise. (6) Therefore, it is my final view that these acts should be done without attachment and having abandoned the desire for the fruits thereof.

(7) The abandonment of any obligatory duty is not proper; such abandonment out of ignorance is declared to be *tāmasic*. (8) He, who abandons action merely because it is difficult, or because of fear it will produce bodily hardship, performs *rājasic* abandonment; and he does not obtain the merit thereof. (9) When action is performed because it is an obligation, merely because it ought to be done, having abandoned attachment and desire for reward, Arjuna, such abandonment is *sāttvic*.

(10) The one who has abandoned—the wise man whose doubt is cut asunder and who is filled with *sattva*—does not hate a disagreeable action, nor is he attached to an agreeable action. (11) For, it is impossible for an embodied being to abandon actions entirely. Therefore, that man, who abandons the fruit of action, is called a man of renunciation. (12) The threefold fruits of action—evil, good, and mixed—accrue after death to those who have not renounced, but never to the one who renounces.

(13) Learn from Me, O Arjuna, the five causes taught in Sāmkhya for the accomplishment of all actions. (14) The seat of action (the body), the doer, the various senses, the different functions of *prāna* (life energy) [enabling the organs and senses], along with the presiding deity. (15) Whatever actions a man performs with his body, speech or mind, whether right or wrong, are caused by these five. (16) This being so, the man of perverse mind, who has not developed his reason, thinks the Self is the doer, but he does not see at all. (17) He, who is free from the notion of egoism and whose understanding is not tainted, though he slays all these men, slays not and is not bound [to the threefold fruits of action].

(18) The threefold impulse of action is knowledge, the object of knowledge, and the knower; the threefold basis of action is the instrument, the action and the doer. (19) Sāmkhya declares that knowledge, action, and agent are of three kinds, distinguished according to the *gunas*. Hear about this also.

(20) Know that knowledge to be *sāttvic* by which one sees one undivided and imperishable existence in all diverse beings. (21) That knowledge which sees diverse beings as separate entities of various kinds is *rājasic*. (22) And, that knowledge which clings to one single effect as if it were the whole—is without reason, without foundation in truth, and insignificant—is declared to be *tāmasic*.

(23) That requisite action performed without attachment, without desire or aversion, by one who seeks no fruit is *sāttvic*. (24) But action which is performed with great effort by one who seeks to gratify his desires and under the prompting of egoism is said to be *rājasic*. (25) That action undertaken because of delusion, disregarding consequences, loss, injury, and ability is declared to be *tāmasic*.

(26) The agent is said to be *sāttvic*, who is free from attachment and self-aggrandizement, endowed with enthusiasm and perseverance, and balanced in success or failure. (27) One who is passionate, desiring the fruits of action, greedy, harmful, impure, and filled with joy and sorrow, such a doer is said to be *rājasic*. (28) The unsteady, vulgar, arrogant, dishonest, malicious, indolent, despondent, and procrastinating agent is *tāmasic*.

(29) Arjuna, I am explaining to you in entirety how distinctions arise as a result of the [predominance of one of the] three *gunas*. Now hear the threefold division of intellect and firmness.

(30) That *buddhi* (the ability to think, reason, and understand—the intellect) which knows when to act and when not to act, what is to be done and what is not to be done, what is to be feared and what is not to be feared, what leads to bondage and what leads to liberation is called *sāttvic*. (31) The intellect which discriminates mistakenly between *dharma* and *adharma* (behaviors that uphold life and those that do not) and that which is to be done and that which is not to be done is *rājasic*, Arjuna. (32) That intellect which, enveloped in darkness, regards wrong to be right, and values all things in a distorted way is *tāmasic*.

(33) That unwavering firmness developed through Yoga (desireless action) by which, the functions of mind, *prāna* (life energy), and senses are restrained, Arjuna, is *sāttvic*. (34) But the firmness, linked with attachment and desire, by which one adheres to duty, enjoyment of pleasures, and earning of wealth, Arjuna, is *rājasic*. (35) That firmness by which a foolish

person does not give up sleep, fear, grief, despair, and also conceit, Arjuna, is *tāmasic*.

(36) And now, Arjuna, I will explain the three kinds of happiness that one enjoys through practice, and by which one comes to the end of suffering. (37) That which is like poison at first, but like nectar in the end; that happiness, arising in a pure intellect cognizing Self, is said to be *sāttvic*. (38) That, which arises from the contact of the senses with the objects of sense, which is like nectar at first but like poison in the end, that pleasure is said to be *rājasic*. (39) And that pleasure which in the beginning and end deludes the self, and which arises from sleep, indolence, and negligence is declared to be *tāmasic*.

(40) There is no being, either on earth or even among the gods in heaven, who is free from these three *gunas* of *prakriti*. (41) The duties of the *brahmins* (priests), the *kshatriyas* (warriors), the *vaiśyas* (merchants), and of the *śūdras* (laborers), Arjuna, are distributed according to the *qualities* arising from their inherent nature. (42) Serenity, self-restraint, austerity, purity, forbearance, uprightness, knowledge, wisdom, and a belief in a hereafter are the duties of *brahmins* born of their inherent nature. (43) Heroism, vigor, steadiness, skill, not fleeing in battle, generosity, and lordliness are the inherent natural duties of the *kshatriyas*. (44) Agriculture, cattle-rearing, and trade are the inherent duties of *vaiśyas*; and the duty of a *śūdras* is service born of their innate nature.

(45) That man who is engrossed in the performance of his own duties attains perfection. Hear how a man acquires perfection by adhering to his own duties. (46) When a man performs the action which befalls him, while worshipping That from whom all beings have evolved and by whom all this is pervaded, he attains perfection. (47) Better is one's own duty, though destitute of merits, than the duty of another well-performed. He who does the duty ordained by his own nature incurs no sin. (48) Arjuna, one should not abandon the duty to which one is born, even though it is attended with evil. Indeed, all undertakings are enveloped by some evil, as fire is by smoke. (49) He whose intellect is not attached to anything, who has self-control, who is free from desires—he, by renunciation [of the fruit of action] attains the supreme state consisting of freedom from action.

(50) Learn from Me in brief, Arjuna, how reaching such perfection one attains *Brahman*, that supreme state of knowledge. (51) With a pure

intellect dwelling [on the Self], firmly restraining the mind, abandoning sound and other objects of senses, and indifferent to attraction and aversion; (52) Resorting to solitude, eating lightly, with speech, body and mind subdued, ever engaged in the yoga of meditation, and taking refuge in dispassion; (53) Having given up egoism, power, arrogance, desire, anger, and possessiveness—peaceful, he becomes worthy for the state of *Brahman*.

(54) Absorbed in *Brahman*, one becomes happy and does not entertain a desire for anything, nor hate anything; regarding all beings alike, he attains supreme devotion to Me. (55) Through devotion, he comes to know me fully—who and what I am in truth—knowing Me in truth, he enters into Me.

(56) Even performing all actions, he, having taken refuge in Me, attains by My grace the eternal, imperishable state. (57-58) Mentally dedicating all actions to Me, having Me as the highest goal, resorting to the yoga of discrimination, and being constantly aware of Me by fixing one's thought on Me, one will overcome all obstacles by My grace. But if one chooses out of egoism not to listen, then they shall perish.

(59) If, filled with egoism, you think, "I shall not fight," your resolve will be in vain. *Prakriti* will compel you. (60) Even against your will, Arjuna, being bound by the action inherently natural to you, you will have to perform that, which by ignorance you do not wish to perform. (61) The Lord abides in the hearts of all beings, Arjuna, spinning them round and round by His divine power as if mounted on a wheel. (62) Seek refuge in Him alone with your whole being, Arjuna. By His grace you shall find supreme peace and the eternal abode. (63) Thus the knowledge, the mystery of mysteries, has been declared to you by Me—reflect on it fully and do what you think best.

(64) Hear again My supreme word, most secret of all. Because you are dearly beloved of Me I will speak to you of what is good. (65) Keep your mind fixed on Me, be devoted to Me, sacrifice to Me, and offer reverence to Me; so shall you come to Me. This is My pledge to you, for you are dear to Me. (66) Give up all other conceptions and take refuge in Me alone. I shall free you from all sins; do not grieve.

(67) This is never to be spoken by you to one who is devoid of austerities, who has no devotion, nor to one who has no desire to listen, nor to one who speaks ill of Me. (68) He who teaches this deeply

profound mystery to My devotees, having performed the highest devotion to Me, shall come to Me without doubt. (69) Nor is there any among men who does dearer service to Me, nor shall there be another on earth dearer to Me, than he.

(70) And he, who will study this sacred dialogue of ours, will be considered by Me as having worshipped Me by the sacrifice of knowledge. (71) And the person who listens to it with faith and without malice, he too shall be released and reach the auspicious realms of those who have performed virtuous deeds.

(72) Has this been heard by you, O Arjuna, with an attentive mind? Has your confusion caused by ignorance been destroyed, Arjuna?

Arjuna said: (73) My delusion is destroyed. I have regained my memory through Your grace, Krishna. I am now free from doubts. I shall act according to Your word.

Sañjaya said: (74) Thus I have heard this dialogue between Krishna and Arjuna, causing my hair to stand on end. (75) By the grace of Vyāsa I have heard this supreme and most profound Yoga which Krishna, the Lord of Yoga, has Himself declared. (76) O King, as I recall again and again this wonderful and holy dialogue between Krishna and Arjuna I rejoice again and again. (77) And remembering that most wonderful cosmic form of the Lord, I am filled with astonishment and joy again. (78) Wherever there is Krishna, the Lord of Yoga, and the archer, Arjuna, there also will be found splendor, victory, prosperity, and righteousness. This is my conviction.

Bibliography

Books based on lectures by Brahmrishi Vishvatma Bawra:

1. Milcetich, William & Margot, editors. *Kapila's Sāmkhya Patanjali's Yoga*, Revised Edition. Brahmrishi Yoga Publications, 2012.

2. Milcetich, William, editor, *Sāmkhya Kārikā with Guadapadacarya Bhāsya*. Brahmrishi Yoga Publications, 2012.

3. Milcetich, William, editor, *The Eternal Soul, Commentary on the Katha Upanishad*. Brahmrishi Yoga Publications, 2009.

4. Milcetich, William, editor, *Yoga in Action*. Brahmrishi Yoga Publications, 2010.

5. Milcetich, William, editor, *Īsa Upanishad, Living in Divinity*. Brahmrishi Yoga Publications, 2012.

Other Books:

1. Adidevananda, Swami, translator. *Śrī Rāmānuja Gītā Bhāsya*. Śrī Rāmākrishna Math, Mylapore, Madras, India, 2001.

2. Chidbhavananda, Swami. *The Bhagavad Gītā*. Sri Ramakrishna Tapovanam, Tiruchirappalli, India, 1991.

3. Ranganathananda, Swami. *The Bhagavad Gītā*, Volumes 1-3. Advaita Ashrama, Kolkata, India, 2000 & 2001.

4. Sargeant, Winthrop, *The Bhagavad Gītā*. Albany, New York: State University of New York Press, 1994.

5. Sastri, A. Mahadeva, translator. *The Bhagavad Gītā with the commentary of Sri Sankaracharya*, Second Edition. Carpentier, Mysore, India, 1901.

6. Satwalekar, P. Shripad Damodar. *Shrimad Bhagawad-Gītā*, Part 1-3. Swadhyaya Mandal, Pardi, India, 1997, 1999 & 2000.

7. Sivananda, Swami. *The Bhagavad Gītā*, Twelfth Edition. The Divine Life Society, Tehri-Garhwal, India, 2008.

8. Tilak, Bal Gangadhar. *Srimad Bhagavadgītā-Rahasya*, Sixth Edition. Pune, India. Geeta Printers, 1986.